David
Smith

Edward F. Fry
and Miranda McClintic

David Smith

Painter Sculptor Draftsman

George Braziller, New York

in association with the

Hirshhorn Museum and

Sculpture Garden

Smithsonian Institution

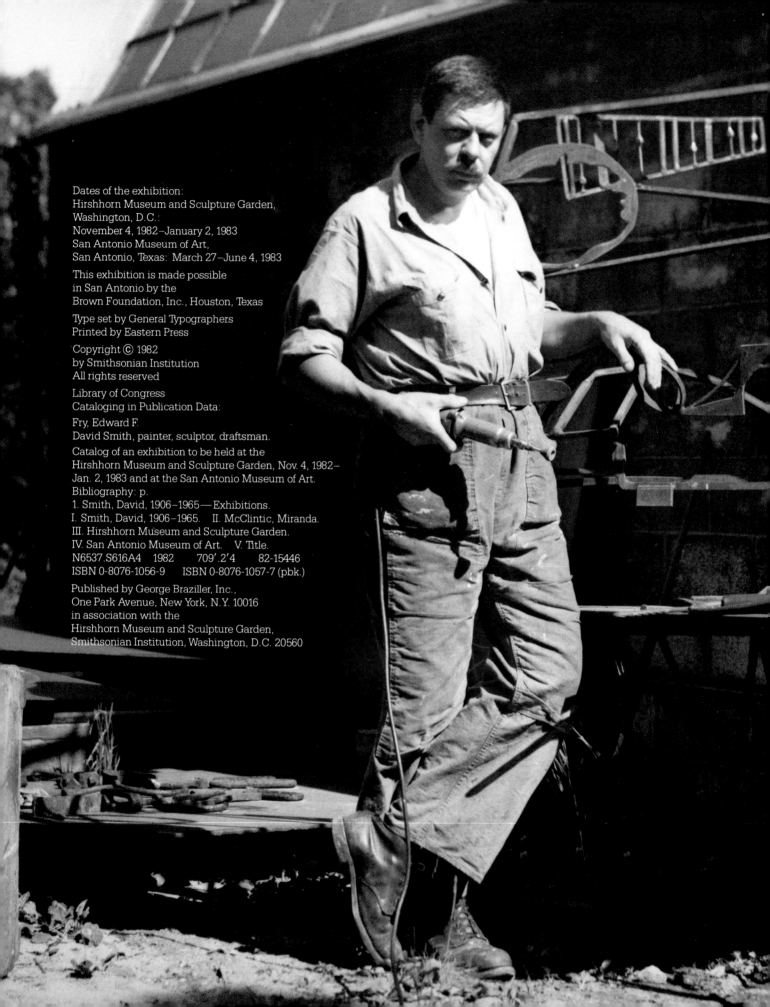

Dates of the exhibition:
Hirshhorn Museum and Sculpture Garden,
Washington, D.C.:
November 4, 1982–January 2, 1983
San Antonio Museum of Art,
San Antonio, Texas: March 27–June 4, 1983

This exhibition is made possible
in San Antonio by the
Brown Foundation, Inc., Houston, Texas

Type set by General Typographers
Printed by Eastern Press

Library of Congress
Cataloging in Publication Data:

Fry, Edward F.
David Smith, painter, sculptor, draftsman.

Catalog of an exhibition to be held at the
Hirshhorn Museum and Sculpture Garden, Nov. 4, 1982–
Jan. 2, 1983 and at the San Antonio Museum of Art.
Bibliography: p.
1. Smith, David, 1906–1965—Exhibitions.
I. Smith, David, 1906–1965.   II. McClintic, Miranda.
III. Hirshhorn Museum and Sculpture Garden.
IV. San Antonio Museum of Art.   V. Title.
N6537.S616A4   1982   709′.2′4   82-15446
ISBN 0-8076-1056-9   ISBN 0-8076-1057-7 (pbk.)

Published by George Braziller, Inc.,
One Park Avenue, New York, N.Y. 10016
in association with the
Hirshhorn Museum and Sculpture Garden,
Smithsonian Institution, Washington, D.C. 20560

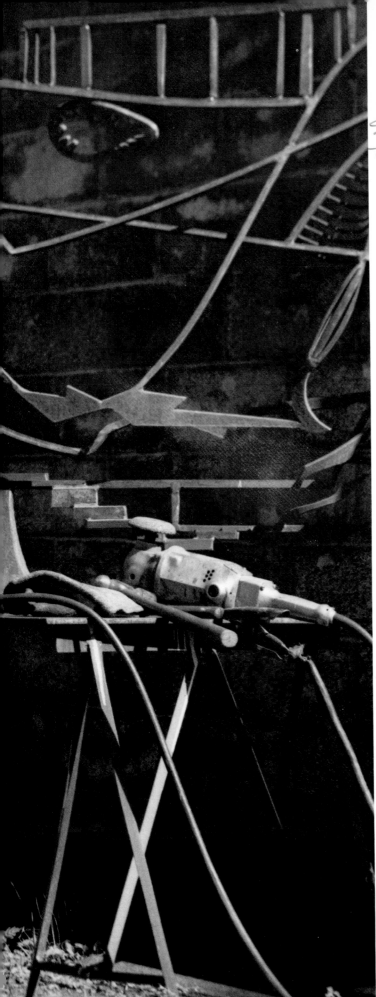

Contents

Lenders to the Exhibition   6

Foreword   8
Abram Lerner

Acknowledgments   9
Miranda McClintic

David Smith: An Appreciation   10
Edward F. Fry

**David Smith:
Painter, Sculptor, Draftsman**   24
Miranda McClintic

Chronology   40

Plates   47

**Annotated Catalog
of the Exhibition**   130

Selected Bibliography   144

Lenders to the Exhibition

Mr. and Mrs. Harry W. Anderson,
    Atherton, California
Janet Bosse, New York
Dorothy Dehner, New York
Ann and Robert Freedman, New York
Dr. Henry Grunebaum, Cambridge, Massachusetts
William J. Hokin, Chicago
Dr. and Mrs. Arthur E. Kahn, New York
Mr. and Mrs. Kenneth Kaiserman, Philadelphia
Mr. and Mrs. David Lloyd Kreeger, Washington, D.C.
Anne Mirvish, Toronto
David Mirvish, Toronto
Muriel Kallis Newman, Chicago
Rita Ransohoff, New York
Rita and Toby Schreiber, Woodside, California
Candida and Rebecca Smith, New York
Frank Stella, New York
Philip T. Warren, Coral Gables, Florida
Two private collections

Albright-Knox Art Gallery, Buffalo, New York
André Emmerich Gallery, New York
Archives of American Art, Smithsonian Institution,
    Washington, D.C.
Des Moines Art Center, Des Moines, Iowa
Folkwang Museum, Essen, Germany
Hirshhorn Museum and Sculpture Garden,
    Smithsonian Institution, Washington, D.C.
Lincoln Center for the Performing Arts, New York
Metropolitan Museum of Art, New York
Museum of Fine Arts, Houston, Texas
Museum of Modern Art, New York
Neuberger Museum, State University
    of New York at Purchase
Saint Louis Art Musem, Saint Louis, Missouri
Storm King Art Center, Mountainville, New York
University Gallery, University of Minnesota,
    Minneapolis
Walker Art Center, Minneapolis
Weatherspoon Art Gallery,
    University of North Carolina at Greensboro
Whitney Museum of American Art, New York

Foreword

In 1979 the Hirshhorn Museum and Sculpture Garden mounted an exhibition of its own holdings of David Smith's sculpture, paintings, and drawings. That exhibition recalled the enthusiasm of Joseph Hirshhorn for Smith's work, which he began to acquire in 1946 and thereafter added to his collection with an avidity that reflected an abiding admiration. In 1966, when Mr. Hirshhorn presented his art collection to the nation, twenty-five works by David Smith were included, a total that has been increased by the acquisition of seven works since 1972. We were aware, in 1979, of the need to do a large and comprehensive survey of Smith's work in the future, and began plans for just such an exhibition, which we are now proud to present.

With the passing years Smith's importance to American art has kept pace with the increasing rarity of his available works, an ironic fact when one considers that of the forty works included in the 1957 Smith exhibition held at the Museum of Modern Art, when the artist was already well known, almost all the sculpture displayed belonged to Smith himself.

By general consensus Smith stands as the hero of American sculpture of the past three decades. All artists hope to be great — Smith achieved greatness through a progression that involved not only his innate talent, but his total dedication, ceaseless hard work, and keen intelligence. Discovering the basic tenets of modernist art before 1930, he subsequently produced works that remain models of aesthetic excellence and continue to serve as guides for generations of sculptors here and abroad.

Smith's art marked a turning point in American sculpture. This exhibition attempts to reveal the complexity of his development as a disciple, innovator, and liberator; it also endeavors to fathom the nature of his contribution, not only as a sculptor, for which he is justly best known, but as a creator whose art embraced all the varieties of media in its effort to arrive at the unified and vigorous statement that characterizes it.

Abram Lerner
Director

Acknowledgments

The number of people it takes to produce a David Smith exhibition is, in a strange way, a testament to the greatness of the man's work. It cannot be easily circumscribed by art history, or set within the bounds of an exhibition and catalog without a struggle.

I sincerely thank everyone who has made this exhibition possible. Smith's daughters, Candida and Rebecca Smith, and Rebecca's husband, Peter Stevens, have a very special understanding of David Smith's work. Their generosity in sharing this with me, and in loaning significant works has been of the utmost importance. M. Knoedler and Company, which represents the Estate of the artist, and Marian Ruggles in particular, helped over and over again. Shirley Matszke, in large part responsible for cataloging the David Smith Estate, supervised the packing and shipping of works loaned by Smith's daughters. Garnett McCoy of the Archives of American Art and several members of his staff have allowed me constant access to the extraordinarily rich David Smith material that has been loaned to the Archives by Candida and Rebecca Smith. A group of Smith's photographs, letters, and notebooks, selected by Mr. McCoy, accompanies this exhibition, and photographs taken by Smith of his sculpture appear throughout the catalog, allowing us to see the pieces through the eyes of their creator. Dorothy Dehner, Smith's wife of twenty years, is one of the finest people I have ever met. Her stories of David Smith have established the historical record of his early work, and, for me, have made his art keenly alive. Edward Fry's interest in David Smith goes at least as far back as the spectacular retrospective exhibition he organized at the Guggenheim Museum in 1969. The insights he provides in this catalog further extend his ideas of that time, and provide a significant contribution to the Smith literature.

The Hirshhorn Museum is full of people who have extraordinary expertise, energy, and good humor. The work on this exhibition by almost everyone in all departments of the institution has been more extensive than usual, and the problems more complicated. I am extremely grateful for the consideration, friendship, and support extended to me during the past year.

Having the benefit of the unfailing graciousness and active involvement of Abram Lerner, the director, has been for me one of the great pleasures of this project. Stephen E. Weil, deputy director, has been supportive in spirit and innovative with his many proposals. Nancy Kirkpatrick, administrator, has been generous with assistance and advice. Charles Millard, chief curator, has more than once shown good faith and extended himself on behalf of the exhibition. This catalog has depended at all stages on the patience, flexibility, and great skill of Virginia Wageman, the Museum's editor. In the curatorial department, Howard Fox, Peggy Gillis, Jill Gollner, and Debbie Geoffray have provided crucial assistance. Doug Robinson and Meryl Muller, as well as all other members of the registrar's department, have been exceedingly patient and painstaking in their arrangements. John Tennant, Lee Stalsworth, and Francie Woltz have been exceptionally involved, in terms of both the quantity and quality of photographs needed for this catalog. Joe Shannon, Eddie Schiesser, Bob Allen, Arthur Courtemanche, and Denise Arnot of the exhibits department are responsible for the superb installation of the exhibition. Missy Sullivan, Gail Kaplan, Frances Betz, and Sophie Orloff — interns at the Museum at different stages of the exhibition's development — provided invaluable assistance with research and a myriad of logistical arrangements. I wish also to thank especially Penine Hart, Charles Bobart, George McDaniels, James Wageman, Jay Smith, Sidney Lawrence, Carol Parsons, Ted Lawson, Victoria Lautman, and Charles Miers for their various contributions.

Above all, my sincere gratitude goes to the many lenders who have allowed us to enjoy their works for a time.

Miranda McClintic

David Smith
An Appreciation

Edward F. Fry

Work and Life

David Smith emerged as an artist at the beginning of the 1930s when, having already settled in New York and having studied at the Art Students League, he began to realize a personal style in drawing, painting, and finally sculpture. His initial efforts reflected both his powerful ambition and his attempts to absorb the visual syntax of European modernism through study of reproductions in European publications and also through such other artists as Matulka, Xceron, and John Graham. During a trip to the Virgin Islands in 1931–32, Smith produced abstracted landscape and still-life paintings and drawings based on a free adaptation of Picasso and surrealist biomorphism, as well as a few reliefs and constructions based on found objects. This sojourn in the Caribbean — the North American equivalent to the Mediterranean world — clarified Smith's previously tentative efforts to translate European modernism into the vernacular of American experience; it also marked a first loosening of the bonds imposed upon Smith by his own Calvinist, Anglo-American, and positivist heritage.

Thus began the grand dialectic underlying the entire work and life of this artist, who is possibly the most perfect exemplar, within the Abstract Expressionist generation to which he belonged, of the interpenetration of European and American traditions. The first fruits of this process appeared in 1933 as a group of welded steel sculptures of heads (K17–19, 21).[1] Here Smith, responding to the example of Picasso's sculptural collaboration with González at the end of the 1920s, welded cast-off fragments of American machinery into cubist-derived representations of human physiognomy. The results were in many ways decisive for Smith's subsequent development. These works signaled his adaptation of American industrial methods and materials to artistic ends; moreover, his eschewal of traditional volumetric sculpture in favor of a frontal, open, and linear mode of representation was based upon draftsmanship and therefore was as applicable to painting as to his nominally three-dimensional sculpture. This underpinning of draftsmanship remained with Smith during his entire life, but in the early and middle 1930s its problematic relationship to European cubist, constructivist, and surrealist sources is of particular interest for what it reveals of the artist's mind and working methods.

Like the slightly older Arshile Gorky, Smith had learned by the mid-1930s to reproduce the external scaffolding of Picasso's cubist *disegno,* as had John Graham earlier. But Smith, more than almost any of his contemporaries, penetrated deeply into the mental processes of cubist representation and absorbed its radical inversion of the classical tradition into his own mind. This absorption of Picasso's visual syntax is profoundly evident in the numerous sculptures of reclining figures Smith made during the mid-1930s (K 20, 38–41, 45, 47, 49, 50) and is all the more remarkable when contrasted with the formalist and generally superficial versions of cubism endemic to American art during much of the period. However, in his paintings of the 1930s, Smith seems at times to have pursued formal interests to a much greater degree — perhaps because of the less demanding nature of the medium — and to have used a drawing or painting as the point of departure for a second, far more formally reductive version of his subject.

Smith went to Europe from the fall of 1936 to mid-1937, during which time he visited contemporary artists in Paris and studied museum collections in various major cities. Among the leading figures of his generation of Abstract Expressionists, he was the only artist other than Gottlieb who actually reached Europe during the 1930s and who thus had direct contact with advanced French art on its native ground. Surviving oil sketches made during this trip reveal Smith's direct contact with, and response to, Parisian surrealist imagery and styles. Among these oil sketches is an untitled 1936 abstraction executed in a purely linear, calligraphic manner: the first in-

1. The letter "K" followed by a number refers to the entries in Rosalind E. Krauss, *The Sculpture of David Smith* (New York: Garland Press, 1977). An illustrated catalogue raisonné, this work is the single most complete and useful factual reference for the artist's work.

stance of this surrealist-inspired method in American art, predating the later well-known examples by half a decade.[2] Although André Masson had exhibited in New York with Pierre Matisse in 1935, and the first publications in English on surrealism had appeared in 1935 and 1936,[3] Smith's drawings and paintings during the middle 1930s represent an independent, direct, and astonishingly precocious response to a crucial aspect of French modernism.

Although Smith was in Europe at the time of Alfred Barr's landmark *Cubism and Abstract Art* exhibition at the Museum of Modern Art in New York, March–April 1936, it would have been impossible for him to have missed the seminal catalog of the exhibition upon his return. Of even greater importance for Smith's development was Barr's second exhibition and accompanying catalog, *Fantastic Art, Dada, Surrealism* (December 1936–January 1937). These two exhibitions and their catalogs, which together were destined to play a far more consequential role than even the Armory Show in the history of American art, had an immediate and lasting effect upon Smith, providing a final impetus to his decade-long apprenticeship to European modernism. There now appear, in addition to Picasso/González-inspired heads and figures, sculptural renditions of still-life motifs derived more or less directly from Picasso paintings of the 1920s, in which Smith's draftsmanship is noticeably formalist and reductive. A second innovation was his depiction of interiors and of landscape, based on Picasso's 1927–28 paintings of artist and model in a studio and above all on Giacometti's *Palace at 4 A.M.*[4] These 1937–39 sculptures differ from earlier

2. Smith's untitled painting (Estate 70.30.35) is in the collection of Candida and Rebecca Smith. For a compilation of other early examples, see Jeffrey Wechsler, *Surrealism and American Art 1931–1947* (New Brunswick, N.J.: Rutgers University Art Gallery, 1977), *passim.*

3. James Thrall Soby, *After Picasso* (New York: Dodd, Mead and Company, 1935); David Gascoyne, *A Short Survey of Surrealism* (1935; reprint ed., London: Cass, 1970); Herbert E. Read, ed., *Surrealism* (London: Faber and Faber, 1936); Julien Levy, *Surrealism* (New York: Black Sun Press, 1936).

4. Picasso's *Atelier* of 1927–28 was acquired by the Museum of Modern Art in 1935, by gift from Walter P. Chrysler, Jr. The *Painter and His Model* of 1928 was included in Barr's *Cubism and Abstract Art* exhibition in 1936 and reproduced in the catalog with a full-page illustration, p. 100. Giacometti's *Palace at 4 A.M.* was reproduced in *Cahiers d'art* in 1932 and was also in Barr's exhibition *Fantastic Art, Dada, Surrealism.* Smith

works in Smith's more willful imposition of stylistic generalization and formal reduction upon his European models, an indication that he found himself somewhat more capable of responding to his sources than before.

A third element in his European apprenticeship was Smith's attempt at purely non-objective sculpture in a quasi-constructivist style (plates 25, 33; K 64, 128–30). These works appeared in the same 1937–39 period as Smith's *Medals for Dishonor,* medallions of social protest against war and capitalism. Indeed, seemingly antithetical preoccupations with pure abstract art and left-wing political themes were characteristic of Smith's generation of New York writers and artists. "Avant-garde" attitudes in social thought and artistic practice were joined together under the banner of Marxist dialectical progressivism in common cause against American bourgeois philistinism.[5] But Smith's few purely non-objective sculptures of the late 1930s share a curious period-piece quality reminiscent less of European constructivism than of the American middle-class utopianism, as manifested in the aesthetic of the 1939 World's Fair.

A final ingredient in Smith's development in the late 1930s was his application of modern European styles to vernacular American themes. Works such as *Billiard Player Construction* (plate 26), *Drummer* (K 54), and *Rooster* (K 72) of 1937, or *Dancer* (K 80) and *Amusement Park* (K 77) of 1938 have their immediate postwar sequels in sculptures of dancing schools, roosters, dancers, and cockfights (plate 77) done in 1945. These works have proved embarrassing to the most ardent of Smith's defenders and are, in many cases, artistic failures. But they are too important to be overlooked, for in them Smith was working as an American artist rather than as a provincial imitator of European high art. Smith's crucial shift from external American iconographic motifs to an internalized American iconology would necessarily take longer to realize, but its point of departure was nevertheless in these homely themes of the late 1930s.

did not see this exhibition, as I erroneously cited in my *David Smith* (New York: Guggenheim Museum, 1969), p. 28, but the work was reproduced in the catalog.

5. For firsthand descriptions of the New York artistic, intellectual, and political atmosphere during the 1930s, see the excellent recent memoir by William Barrett, *The Truants: Adventures among the Intellectuals* (New York: Anchor Press, 1982).

During World War II, Smith remained in upstate New York more or less continuously, doing war work in a factory in Schenectady and occasionally visiting his farm at Bolton Landing, near Lake George. He was thus effectively isolated from the world of modern art, not only from the effects of war upon European cultural life but also, by his absence from New York City, from the impact of European refugee artists and intellectuals on his American contemporaries. (After 1940 Smith would in fact never again live in New York City, apart from periodic short visits.) A further degree of isolation was caused by Smith's lack of time and materials to make sculpture. The war period was thus a time of narrowed horizons, severed links, and, of necessity, turning inward upon personal resources; it was also the crucible that made David Smith a great artist. He turned more than ever before to drawing and printmaking, and began to explore and confront his inner psychic pressures even as he saw the full human and historical tragedy of the war itself.

The result was that rarest of all events in the modern tradition, an authentically new iconography that is both personal and public. In a series of drawings, etchings, and notebook sketches dating from the end of the 1930s to the mid-1940s, Smith brought images descended from his work on the *Medals for Dishonor* into juxtaposition with cannons and various other instruments of war (plate 9). But he was beginning to confront his own internal world at the same time; and there he found a profound ambivalence toward women, as both objects of desire and threatening, emasculating predators (K 733, 797, 808, 815–22). This tension may be labeled oedipal or sadomasochistic, but it should also be recognized as an almost inevitable consequence of Smith's puritanical American heritage, further complicated by the loneliness and marital difficulties of a brilliantly ambitious, powerful, yet sensitive man. Although it is a prescription for the classic American tragedy of stifled dreams and withered emotions, Smith prevailed; out of the disturbing imagery of his demon women and phallic cannons, and from his search for symbolic and formal models in the European tradition — notably surrealism — he brought his art and his life together in a group of extraordinary sculptures done in 1945–46. In *Spectre Riding the Golden Ass* (1945; K 189),

imagery of hermaphroditic winged phalluses appears, while in other works, such as *Rape* (1945; K 185), cannons rape prostrate women: a fusion of public history and private obsessions. But also in 1945, with *Reliquary House* (K 186), *Home of the Welder* (plate 52), and *Pillar of Sunday* (K 184), David Smith gained access to a new level of symbolic discourse.[6] With these works he externalized his psychic conflicts by using European models, above all Giacometti, as vehicles for his own symbolic language, which was wrought out of his confrontation with the self. These pivotal works of the mid-1940s are among the least known of Smith's achievements, but they are masterpieces. For here the artist performed a multivalent rite of passage, in which he shifted from the external, stylistic mimicry of European models to their translation and redeployment for subjective, American, and romantic/cathartic ends, in which the making of art became a life-saving necessity rather than the embellishment of an already rich, venerable, and distant tradition.

Smith was still working on a small, almost intimate scale in the mid-1940s, in keeping not only with financial considerations but also with the symbolic function of his sculptures, which require "reading" in much the same way as do the complex allegories of a Dürer print or the cryptic drawings in Smith's own sketchbooks. But his interests, both iconographically and formally, began to expand rapidly in the immediate postwar years. Thus, if in *Steel Drawing I* of 1945 (plate 57) he paid homage simultaneously to Picasso's draftsmanship of the 1920s and to the style of Mondrian,[7] he could also in the 1946 *Spectre of Mother* (K 210) translate both the form of Giacometti's 1933 sculpture *Taut Thread* and the surrealist use of the oedipal myth into the most extreme and explicit of all his confrontations with self and past. In this work the mother, with pendulous breasts, devours a phallic presence like a praying mantis after mating, while the postcoital winged male spirit hangs lifeless and inverted beneath the maternal lures of home-

6. See Fry, *David Smith*, pp. 40–45, for detailed iconographic analyses; see also Krauss, *Sculpture of David Smith*, pp. 32–35, for additional information and interpretation.

7. A Mondrian commemorative exhibition was held at the Museum of Modern Art, New York, March 21–May 13, 1945, following the artist's death the previous year.

baked pies and doughnuts.[8] But this work, with its all too vivid private symbolism, was the last instance of such explicitness; by comparison, a group of symbolic works done in 1950, *The Letter* (K 232), *Cathedral* (K 229), and *Sacrifice* (K 235), reveals little overt symbolic discourse, relying instead on the more generalized iconographies of dramatic situations. For in the intervening years of the later 1940s, Smith moved beyond even the internalizing of his surrealist models, and as the direct influence of European art receded, he gradually turned toward the central theme of American consciousness: the relation of the lone individual to nature and to the vastness of earth and sky.

Smith began to make sculptures based on landscape in 1946, beginning with such works as the Miró- and Tanguy-inspired *Helmholtzian Landscape* (plate 46) and culminating with *Hudson River Landscape* (fig. 8) of 1951, his masterpiece in this genre. Of even greater importance to Smith than landscape, however, was the relationship of earth to sky and, in particular, the individual's unmediated relationship to the universe. Smith's approach to this fundamental expression of the Protestant imagination went through several stages, beginning with iconographic references to air and flight. *Royal Bird* (plate 82), *Eagle's Lair* (plate 37), and *Portrait of the Eagle's Keeper* (K 227), all of 1948–49, share the theme of flight as well as a possible veiled reference to the predatory aspects of traditional social structures.

Yet, just as Smith's landscape theme reached fruition in the early 1950s, so did his iconography of earth and sky receive its fullest expression in three major works, beginning with *Star Cage* (plate 73) of 1950. In this sculpture, Smith clearly tried to make a link between the earth and the sky by creating a metaphorical image of the heavens and placing it upon a narrow, upwardly thrusting pyramidal base. In *Fish* (K 230) of 1950–51, he used the less direct metaphor of weightlessness in water, supporting his cubist/surrealist image once again on a tall, narrow base in midair. Finally, in *Australia* (plate 83) of 1951, he returned to the image of flight and in this monumental masterpiece made his definitive statement, not only of the iconography of flight itself but of the consequent linking of earth and sky. For in *Australia*, the huge insectlike bird is barely touching earth, as though to pause before soaring; and atop its linear structure is a sign of clouds in the sky, used summarily in *Hudson River Landscape* but clearly visible in drawings made for *Star Cage*.[9] *Australia*, in its disembodied linearity and its generalized iconography of the linking of earth and sky, thus represents Smith's first supremely realized expression of the American iconology of Protestant transcendence, an iconologic intention that is also revealed in the way Smith photographed this and other works of related theme: against the sky and seen from below so that the image itself seems to rest upon the top of a distant hillside.

The years 1949 to 1951 were a watershed both in Smith's work and in his life. As an artist, he had moved gradually away from the particularities of his iconographic obsessions of the mid-1940s; and he was also developing a style that responded less to its sources in the fine-grained mental structures of his European mentors than to his personal version of American consciousness. His personal lyricism is already evident in *Blackburn: Song of an Irish Blacksmith* (1949–50; K 228) and the ironically elegaic *Letter* (1950; K 232); but conversely, in 1951, he also paid final homage to his absorption of Picasso's cubist representation in *Banquet* (K 246) and acknowledged his indebtedness to Giacometti in *All around the Square* (K 242) and *Stainless Window* (K 262). This last work is a curious reprise of such earlier responses to Giacometti as Smith's 1939 *Interior for Exterior* (K 122). Another similarly formalized restatement at this time was possibly the otherwise enigmatic *Question and Answer* (1951; K 260), which bears a curiously reductive relationship to the 1946 *Spectre of Mother*.

It was also in the early 1950s that Smith began to receive greater recognition for his work than before, as signaled by a Guggenheim fellowship in 1950,

8. For this iconography, see the sketchbook drawings for *Reliquary House* in Fry, *David Smith*, pp. 44–45, figs. 24A, 24B; also illustrated in Krauss, *Sculpture of David Smith*, figs. 807, 812a.

9. See Krauss, *Sculpture of David Smith*, figs. 743 (slightly cropped at the top) and 744. Both drawings were exhibited in 1979 at the Whitney Museum of American Art; see the accompanying catalog by Paul Cummings, *David Smith: The Drawings*, nos. 34 and 31 respectively, with an illustration of the latter on p. 66.

which was renewed in 1951; and it was also at this time that his first marriage was coming to an end. Along with great changes in his personal life, the decade of the 1950s proved to be a period of restless experimentation and of searching for a new expressive language, rather than one of steady accomplishment. Nevertheless, in addition to his remarriage in 1953 to a younger woman, and to his greatly increased public activity (including many exhibitions, lectures, and teaching stints in Midwestern colleges), Smith made over two hundred sculptures in this decade—almost as many as he had completed altogether in the years leading up to 1950. But this enormous output still included such older preoccupations as the iconography of birds in flight (a series of *Ravens,* plate 95 and K 380, 429, 468, 469; the 1959 *Study in Arcs,* plate 106) and a continuation of his interest in refining the cubist language of Picasso and González. Certain works of the 1950s are, in fact, almost textbook examples of cubist signification, notably *Agricola VIII* (1952; K 272), *Coil Spring* (1953; K 287), *Agricola 54* (1954; K 319), *Sitting Printer* (1954; K 328), *Sentinel II* (1957; K 430), and above all *Lonesome Man* (1957; plate 87). In certain instances, Smith was clearly returning to earlier European models for renewed guidance, as is evident in the close formal derivation of *Agricola IV* (1952; K 268) from a photograph in his possession of a sculpture by González (ill. K 789).

Accompanying these formally reductive reprises of prior stylistic sources was a radical diminution of Smith's iconographic references to only a handful of motifs, of which the most important was his appropriation of the traditional sculptural theme of the freestanding figure. With *Agricola I* (K 264) and *The Hero* (K 256), both of 1951–52, Smith announced at the very beginning of the decade the motif that he would pursue to the end: the heroically isolated individual, confronting no human or social situation but simply the vastness of nature itself. Smith rang the changes on this theme through a wide range of styles and methods, from the pure cubism of *The Hero* itself or the later *Lonesome Man* (1957), to the cubist assemblage of *Coil Spring* (1953), *Sitting Printer* (1954), *History of Leroy Borton* (1956; K 371), *Sentinel II* (1957), *Sentinel III* (1957; fig. 7), and *XI Books III Apples* (1959; K 465), to the sheer graphic verticality of the 1955 *Forging* series (K 333–42). Occasionally Smith underscored the masculinity of his heroes with an overtly phallic sign, as in *Tanktotem V* (1955–56; K 384) and, as he would do in the 1960s also, in the verbal-visual phallic pun in *Voltri Bolton I* (1962; K 585). This race of lonely heroes assumed a new guise during the later 1950s in *Five Units Equal* (1956; K 368), *Four Units Unequal* (c. 1960; K 489), and *5½* (c. 1956; K 367) where, despite his experimentation with hollow steel modules, the iconographic motif and expressive purpose remained unchanged.

Like the overwhelming majority of Smith's sculptures, these male images of the 1950s were made of steel and were either life size or slightly larger in scale. The artist made another group of life-size vertical figures which, according to their imagery and often their titles, are representations of women: *Portrait of a Painter* (1954; K 326), *Portrait of a Young Girl* (1954; K 327), *Detroit Queen* (1957; K 417), and *Auburn Queen* (1959; plate 91). Smith's working method in these female figures is significant, for he used bronze instead of steel. It is as though in his mind the latter material, which is tough, difficult to use, and requires welding, was associated with the male gender and with sculpture itself; while bronze, being more easily shaped and manipulated, had a gentler, feminine character, which he also associated with traditional sculpture and with the less resistant medium of painting.

Although a prominent subject in his work, Smith's race of male heroes and their bronze consorts were not his only preoccupation during the 1950s. He was also experimenting with a variety of materials and working methods, many of which were, like his residual cubism and surrealism, remnants of his earlier ties to French modernism. The most conspicuous of these experiments was his use of found objects, be they parts of agricultural equipment in the *Agricola* series or ends of boiler tanks in the *Tanktotems;* in these as in other comparable instances, the name of the series refers to the materials used rather than to iconographic intentions and has no other intrinsic significance. But Smith's development of sculptural series during the 1950s is in itself significant, for there is an exact relationship between the greater quantity of the works he produced and the diminution of iconographic complexity, in favor of the simple iconographic type or motif. Some of the small-scale works in these series, notably the *Albanys* of the late 1950s and early 1960s and, to a lesser extent, the *Menands* of the 1960s, were essentially sketches carried out in steel rather than on paper. Many of these same small-scale works, like a large proportion of the non-figurative sculptures of the period, display a marked degree of formalist reductiveness in both style and iconography when compared to their sources.

Out of this heterogeneous production, with its increasing formalism and diminished iconographic specificity, emerged two themes of sufficient importance to bear comparison with Smith's race of heroes and heroines. The first was a tendency toward dematerialization, which was an expected consequence of Smith's long-term commitment to a personal version of cubism, with its inevitably linear, frontal, and pictorial consequences. But what was linear and pictorial in *Hudson River Landscape* (fig. 8), *Banquet,* or *Australia* (plate 83) in the early 1950s was also highly inflected with specific iconographies; whereas the dematerialization that emerged during the later 1950s was a formal theme which, although virtually devoid of iconography, nevertheless became an iconologic statement in itself. What Smith did was simply to discover that highly reflective surfaces not only opticalize and pictorialize sculpture but also cause it to appear to be as immaterial as light itself. He began this new approach to materials with experiments where he used sterling silver as a sculptural medium in the mid-1950s, but by 1955–56 he also turned to using polished stainless steel; and by 1959–60, in such works as *XI Books III Apples* and *Five Units Unequal,* he had fused this new iconological theme of dematerialization with his older iconography of the isolated hero. Smith also painted his sculptures during this period, as he had done sporadically since the 1930s, and he even applied paint to the steel surfaces of *Five Units Equal* (1956) and the reworked composition *5½* (c. 1956). But this literal pictorialization of sculpture, seen also in many of his works of the 1960s, came close at times to the rematerialization of Smith's sculptures as physical variants of contemporary hard-edge painting (as in *Tanktotem VII,* 1960; K 494).

Of greater interest is the second of Smith's new themes to emerge during the 1950s, which might best be described as levitation. A lineal descendant (by way of mental reductiveness) of Smith's earlier iconography of flight that had culminated in *Australia* of 1951 (plate 83), this iconologic theme of levitation appeared tentatively in the painted *Lunar Arcs on One Leg* (1956–60; K 491) but soon reached full expression in two important works, *8 Planes 7 Bars* of 1957–58 (K 445) and *Fifteen Planes* (fig. 11) of 1958 (K 446), which are both made of stainless steel and are far taller than a human figure. In these two sculptures, Smith achieved the effect of compositional elements weightlessly floating in the air, supported as if incidentally by an understructure; it is the dramatic situation of *Australia* again, but with all iconographic references distilled to an essence. Similarly, the extreme linear openness of *Australia* is now restated through a greater sense of dematerialization achieved by emphasizing the reflective qualities of stainless steel. Thus these two great iconologic inventions of the 1950s begin to merge at the end of the decade; and the iconography of the isolated hero of the early 1950s undergoes a metamorphosis and emerges within the mind and body of David Smith himself, who reaches upward toward the infinite sky with the power of his plastic imagination.

By the end of the 1950s Smith had thus completed the transformation of his earlier motifs into generalized gestures, stances, and attitudes, which were now as reductive iconographically as were the formal properties of his sculptures themselves. In place of heroes and of images of flight, there was now the internalized restatement of these themes in a manner that is immediately recognizable as romantic transcendentalism. Accompanying this shift was a remarkable increase both in the scale and ambition of his sculptures and in the relative speed and quantity of their production. Yet a certain degree of détente is apparent in Smith's work at the beginning of the 1960s. It was a period during which he was divorced from his second wife, but also when he established close friendships with artists of a younger generation, notably Kenneth Noland (b. 1926) and Anthony Caro (b. 1926), who were both living in nearby Bennington, Vermont. Almost a full generation younger

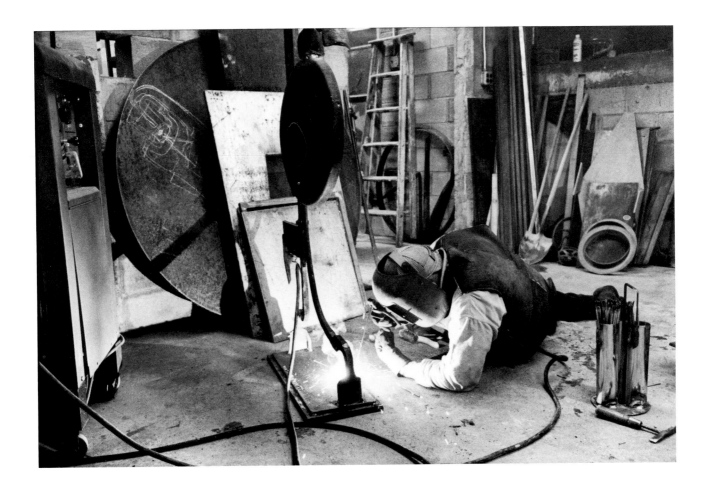

than Smith, these artists and their contemporaries, championed by Smith's old friend the critic Clement Greenberg and his followers, were committed to an antitranscendental yet residually romantic phenomenalism. Their art was characterized by a highly formal approach, with sharp edges, geometrical forms, and flat uninflected color. It was an aesthetic that would become the dominant mode of the 1960s in America, and it also had a strong, if limited, effect on Smith's own work at the beginning of the decade.

The younger generation's influence on Smith was most strikingly evident in his increased interest in painting his sculptures in 1960–62 and in his employment of simple, rectilinear forms for most of his work during the last five years of his life. Smith also directly borrowed the motif of the circle from Noland's paintings of the late 1950s and early 1960s. These Noland circles, painted in flat clear hues, appeared

explicitly in such works as *Circles Intercepted* (1961; K 510), *Circles I, II,* and *III* (1962; K 547–49), *2 Circles 2 Crows* (1963; K 626), *Zig VII* (1963; K 627), and *Zig VIII* (1964; K 641). Yet this repictorialization of a sculpture that was already pictorial and also optically dematerialized was a dead end for Smith, whose formal and expressive powers far exceeded the more modest gifts and ambitions of Noland, Caro, and other contemporary practitioners of 1960s formalist manner. Despite this detour into color and a hard-edge aesthetic, Smith's thematic concerns remained intact; for aside from their polychromed rectilinearity, such works as *Three Planes* (1960–61; K 499), *Hicandida* (1961; K 515), and *Zigs I* and *II* (1961; K 531, 532) are monumentalized revivals of Smith's cubist-inflected lonely heroes of the 1950s. Even *Zig IV* (1961; plate 111), one of the most enigmatic of Smith's later works, is a revival of Smith's obsession during the early 1940s with both the Giacomettesque tableau and the imagery of cannons, here translated into reductive cubist syntax and presented with a discontinuity between the levitated structure and its support.

The European sources that so successfully nourished Smith during the 1930s and 1940s are even more evident in the series of *Voltris* that he made during the month of June 1962 in Italy. There, suddenly removed from his own surroundings, sculptures, and friends, Smith revealed the essential motivating influences on his work. These pieces were predominantly depictions of standing human figures and were based on signification derived from cubism, with found objects used in the manner of giant steel collages. A number of important influences on his work, including childhood experiences, apprenticeship at the Terminal Iron Works in Brooklyn, wartime work on tanks and locomotives, and Giacometti's tabletop tableaux, resonate in the imagery of workbenches and giant wheeled wagons; and his recent involvement with Noland's circle motif is also manifested in many of these Italian works.

Smith continued this Italian mode during later 1962 and early 1963, after his return to America, with a series of sculptures entitled variously *Voltri Bolton, Volton,* or simply *VB* that incorporated steel parts and tools he had brought back with him (plate 116). As in Italy, the predominant theme was the standing figure, with occasional references to Noland and Giacometti. But the major focus of his work between 1962 and his accidental death in 1965 was his series of *Cubis,* a group of almost thirty monumental sculptures in which he returned to his earlier discovery of the dematerializing reflective quality of polished stainless steel. Assembled from modular units of hollow steel boxes and composed according to spray-painted sketches and mockups of empty milk and liquor cartons, the *Cubis* mark Smith's extension of the transcendental iconology of his maturity and the continuing development of his image of the lonely hero.

Cubi I (K 649) of early 1963, one of the supreme masterpieces of the series, of Smith's entire career, and of modern sculpture as a whole, is a brilliant conflation of the artist's thematic and stylistic inventions. It is a standing figure of heroic scale, reaching up-

ward toward the sky; with its subtly unbalanced construction it achieves the effect of weightlessness; and with its polished reflective surface it is dematerialized and so has the purity of a transcendental gesture. More explicitly levitational is another masterpiece, *Cubi XVII* (K 665), also of 1963, in which, like the contemporary *5 Ciarcs* (K 614) and *Tower I* (K 625) and the 1964 *Cubis XVIII, XIX,* and *XX* (fig. 4; K 666, 668), an invisible psychic gesture has seemingly raised matter skyward. These structures — like "square clouds," as Smith referred to the earliest *Cubi* [10] — float as if suspended between heaven and earth, as did the great bird of *Australia* a decade earlier.

The motif of the hero returns in 1964–65 with renewed grandeur, both as externalized image and as internalized, subjective vision. Like *Cubi I, Cubis XXII* (1964; K 670) and *XXV* (1965; K 673) are monumental figures, standing with arms widespread. Similarly, *Becca* (1965; plate 115) confronts the universe with the defiant gesture of an Ahab or of Goya's martyred hero in the *Execution of the 3rd of May 1808.* But the hero within the artist is expressed in the last *Cubis:* he leaves his footprints in the giant strides of *Cubi XXIII* (1964; fig. 9) and the even more kinesthetically expressive *Cubi XXVI* (1965; fig. 6); and Smith finally built gateways worthy of a hero's passage in *Cubis XXIV* (1964; K 672), *XXVII* (1965; K 675), and *XXVIII* (1965; K 676). With these works and with tragic unexpectedness, ended the odyssey of an artist whose career, beginning with the awkward and painful struggles to make sculpture out of bits of coral, wood, and discarded machinery a quarter century earlier, was itself almost larger than life.

David Smith and Modernism in America
As a man and as an artist David Smith was destined by circumstance, and by his own talents, intelligence, and will power, to become a supreme exemplar of the modern artist in America. He was blessed by fate even to the time and place of his birth, in 1906 and in the Middle West. He was thus imbued with self-confident innocence and no longer compelled, as was the previous generation, to seek inspiration

10. Cited by Krauss, *Sculpture of David Smith,* p. 116.

abroad as an expatriate. Like virtually all the greatest creators of the twentieth century, he was a provincial, driven by ambition to reach the highest levels of achievement rather than to consume the visions of others.

Smith's generation was too young to die in the First World War and too old, for the most part, to see combat in the Second. As an artist he also came of age in the late 1920s and early 1930s in time to fall heir not only to European cubism and constructivism but to surrealism as well. Because of the Depression of the 1930s, he was forced to assimilate European modernism for the most part at a distance, and therefore imperfectly, within the context of American life and sensibility: his was the generation of the Abstract Expressionists; like them he would effect a uniquely powerful transformation of the modern tradition.

Smith has always been linked with Abstract Expressionism, particularly in his later work. Formal parallels can be made between Abstract Expressionist paintings and his sculptures, and even more so with his drawings and paintings. His ink drawings of the 1950s in particular, with their superb, almost calligraphic brushwork and overall automatist style (plate 81), are close in manner to the gouaches of Kline and de Kooning of the same period. Smith's career was also linked to Abstract Expressionism not only in time but also through circumstance. He began as a painter and was active in New York art circles throughout the 1930s. Like so many Abstract Expressionist painters, he studied at the Art Students League, haunted the galleries where advanced French art was shown, and studied the reproductions in *Cahiers d'art* and other periodicals. Like Pollock, de Kooning, and many other American artists of the 1930s, Smith was virtually obsessed with Picasso; and he knew from an early date not only Gorky, de Kooning, and other Abstract Expressionists but also John Graham, the catalytic *éminence grise* of the Paris–New York axis. Nevertheless, there remains a question that is almost never raised in critical and historical discourse: was David Smith an Abstract Expressionist? If not, what was his art; and if so, what is Abstract Expressionist sculpture? The answers to these questions demand that the essential formal, iconographic, and historical qualities of Abstract Ex-

pressionist painting be considered; and that the relation of painting to sculpture in Abstract Expressionism — its *paragone* — be determined.

The significant Abstract Expressionist painters, de Kooning, Gorky, Newman, Pollock, Rothko, and Still, underwent a similar set of formative experiences that led to their ultimate achievements. All passed through a long period of provincial apprenticeship, during the 1930s and 1940s, to the two final phases of the European classical tradition: the cubist phenomenology of cognition of objects through a self-conscious reinvention of representation, and the surrealist phenomenology of mind through the self-conscious exploration of the various modes of consciousness itself. This apprenticeship was undertaken by young artists who, with the partial exceptions of the foreign-born Gorky and de Kooning, came to the encounter with European modernism from cultural formations that were in most cases non-urban, non-cosmopolitan, and Protestant/puritanical (Still being the extreme case). The response of these young artists to cubism and surrealism was at first that of a formalized mimicry of styles and methods, in which the secret life of European art was fathomed from its exterior visual skin rather than from its intentions, to which the Americans had no access. It is nevertheless ironic that those cultivated and cosmopolitan Americans who did, in fact, have such access — A. E. Gallatin, George L. K. Morris — succeeded only in becoming colonial practitioners of European high modernism; for they lacked that gritty independence and desperate ambition that their Abstract Expressionist compatriots brought to bear upon the seductive prestige of Paris.

In the midst of this apprenticeship to the formal skin of European modernism, the Abstract Expressionists then turned toward inward concerns. In part, this shift was instigated by the growing influence of surrealism and its mythic iconography during the later 1930s, culminating in the arrival of the artists themselves in America during their wartime exile. But in part this inward shift also occurred with several artists as the unavoidable consequence of psychic pressures and urgencies, ranging from the intense puritanism of Still to the personal anguish of Gorky, the metaphysical unrest of Newman and

Rothko, and the emotional turmoil of Pollock. These artists alone, among all the Abstract Expressionist painters, thus reached a crisis point at which internal pressures exerted an equal and opposing force to the external cultural authority of European modernism. From about 1944–45 until the beginning of the 1950s these American painters, each in his own way, resolved the conflict in his life and art by using European artistic means for personal, non-European, non-classical ends. The artist's interior pressures were projected outward upon the picture surface, there to meet the formal and iconographic heritage of European modernism; the two opposing forces fused, in the process transforming each other and resulting in Abstract Expressionist painting.

The first stage of this extraordinary dialectical process was the transformation of classically based surrealist myths into personal terms, as is seen in the work of Gorky, Pollock, and Rothko between 1942 and 1945. The second and final stage was the reductive metamorphosis of subjective myths and symbols into an even purer and more generalized relationship between the individual psyche and the world; in this final phase of Abstract Expressionism, which emerged by circa 1947–49 in Pollock, Rothko, Newman, and Still, the formal and stylistic means of European modernism were also purified and generalized. The painting that resulted from this final transformation of both iconography and style was, with its total absorption and metamorphosis of European sources, once again American in essence, heroic in scale, purged of classical hierarchy, and ascetic almost to the point of puritanism. Its precedents in American art were the vast landscape paintings of the nineteenth century; and its epistemology, also like the nineteenth century, was the unequal relationship between the individual and the awesomeness of nature. This "abstract sublimity" of Abstract Expressionist painting may thus be understood to be a radical revision of the indigenous American Protestant iconology of romantic transcendentalism.

From this historical and critical perspective, the relationship of David Smith to Abstract Expressionism emerges with a new clarity. Smith, first of all, underwent exactly the same phases of development as did his fellow painters, from apprenticeship to European art during the 1930s, to the translation of style and symbol into personal terms during the 1940s, to a formal purified iconology of Protestant transcendentalism in the 1950s and 1960s. But Smith's ambiguous role as both a painter and a sculptor, whose sculptures nevertheless approached non-sculptural pictorialism, has obscured the true stature of his artistic achievement. The turning point in his work was in 1950–52: by then he had developed his sculptural equivalent of cubist/surrealist pictorial vision to a limit and had recast it in personal terms in such works as *Banquet* and *Hudson River Landscape* (fig. 8). After these works, it was his stroke of genius to raise that vision from the horizontal gaze suitable for landscape or its pictorial equivalent, and to redirect it upward toward the sky. *Star Cage* (plate 73) marked a crucial first step in this change; but *Australia* (plate 83) was the pivotal work in his entire career, for it stands at the end of a long iconographic and stylistic evolution and at the beginning of a new dematerialized yet monumental expression of the vertical relation between earth and sky.

Smith's subsequent development of the motif of the lone hero was the penultimate step in his art, for through his heroes Smith, as well as the viewer, empathetically enters into a confrontation with the universe. Finally, in the *Cubis,* Smith reached a radical generalization of his subjective viewpoint accompanied by a purification of stylistic means, which together were the exact equivalents of what Pollock and his contemporaries had achieved a decade earlier. But where the painters had created monumental canvases, in front of which they and their audience could experience the transcendental metaphor of the individual confronting an infinite landscape of the mind, Smith went further and in effect challenged the very awesomeness of nature itself. For he accepted the sky and the earth as what they are: the inescapable, overarching canvas within which the human drama is enacted. But into the place of the spectator passively contemplating such a canvas, be it nature or art, Smith thrust the creations of his mind and hands; his *Cubis* are metaphors of an active human force which does not simply acknowledge the emptiness of the universe, but defies it.

What Smith began in 1950–52, when he raised his

imagination and imagery from a horizontal pictorialism to a vertical emphasis, was the liberation of his sculpture from the conditions of Abstract Expressionist painting, which by 1950 had reached its inevitable romantic endpoint in the iconic realm. No sculpture, no matter how purified and pictorialized, could compete with painting under such conditions; but only Smith, of all the sculptors of his generation, would grasp this dilemma and create a new kind of sculpture that in its vertical transcendence would equal, if not surpass, in the power of its iconologic effect, the greatest paintings of the period.

Thus, the problem Smith faced was that of the *paragone:* the relation of painting to sculpture, and the proper role and function of each medium. Within the framework of Abstract Expressionism this question is rarely if ever raised; but the *paragone* in this version of romantic art, and its relation to the classical *paragone*[11] are issues too important to be ignored. Within the post-medieval classical tradition, the highest function to which the isolated easel painting may aspire is the allegorical: the conflation of past and future narrative/symbolic discourse into a present moment which, by virtue of the non-temporal nature of painting, is thereby the richest and most complete role for that medium. By contrast, sculpture, when it is sculpture and not — as in relief, or in niche or tableau assemblages of figures — painting in disguise, attains its highest function as symbol: the concentrated incarnation of values and ideals in a single isolated figure or group, in which narrative may, rarely, be implied but which nevertheless functions in its totality as a single symbolic statement.

It is much more difficult to establish a *paragone* for romantic art, let alone Abstract Expressionism; for in the latter, time, narration, and the relation of the past and future to the present hardly play a role as they do in classicism. Romantic art, including the American landscape tradition and the radical restatement of

that tradition in Abstract Expressionist painting, is almost always drawn to a transcendental absolute that exists beyond space and time. Thus, the most adequate function for such romantic painting always approaches the iconic, which in comparison to classical allegory is a less complex use of the medium, just as romantic transcendentalism itself is a simple and almost primitive approach to the world in comparison to that of the classic. But the later works of Smith, though dedicated to the Abstract Expressionist goal of romantic transcendence, are monumental sculptures that symbolically express and incarnate the romantic ideals of transcendence. Smith's use of the sculptural medium is therefore directly comparable in its completeness to the symbolic incarnation of values in classical sculpture. But if Smith invented what was probably the sole authentic mode for Abstract Expressionist sculpture, and if he gave new vitality to the traditional symbolic function of the sculptural medium, he also maintained in his *Cubis* and other late works a tense ambiguity between sculptural volume and pictorial reflectivity; in effect, he raised to a vertical axis that same sculptural/pictorial conflation that he had practiced a dozen years before in *Hudson River Landscape* and similar works. The real dilemma of an Abstract Expressionist *paragone,* therefore, is that a purely sculptural expression of romantic transcendence may not be possible, Smith's *Cubis* and Newman's *Broken Obelisk* being the only exceptions. Hegel's conclusion that painting is the principal medium of the fine arts in the modern romantic period is apparently confirmed.

The full recognition of the stature of Smith's achievement has only begun. Like most of his Abstract Expressionist contemporaries, he has suffered since his death at the hands of artists and critics who have imposed a truncated and formalist misreading upon him. His works became an implicit point of departure for a generation of sculptors who rose to prominence in the 1960s and who saw Smith's sculptures as formal objects and relations, but who avoided their iconologic intentions. The extent of this misreading became evident as early as 1966 with the public awareness of Donald Judd's wall sculptures of

11. For the most recent treatment of the *paragone* (the comparison of artistic media) in European art, see the excellent study by Leatrice Mendelsohn, *Paragoni: Benedetto Varchi's Due Lezzioni and Cinquecento Art Theory* (Ann Arbor: UMI Research Press, 1982).

metallic boxes and their problematic relationship to Smith's *Cubis.* Only one critic at the time asked the fundamental question about Judd's boxes: whether or not they were physically or perceptually hollow.[12] The total pertinence of such a question to Judd's phenomenologically based work underscores the distance between it and the *Cubis,* to which all such issues are ultimately irrelevant. Similarly, Smith's friend Caro made during the late 1960s sculptures incorporating materials, such as bits of agricultural equipment and boiler tank ends, which were identical in type to those used earlier by Smith himself. But in works like Caro's 1969–70 *Sun Feast,*[13] the divergence of these two artists is mutually illuminating. Where Smith would assemble found objects into images of the hero or motifs of levitation, Caro's goal was earthbound and phenomenalist: the dematerialization of steel through color and compositional artifice for the purpose of raising sculpture from the ground to the level of the viewer's perceptual and cognitive

12. Leo Steinberg; at a public symposium held at the Jewish Museum, New York, 1966, on the occasion of the exhibition *Primary Structures* dedicated to recent minimalist sculpture.

13. Illustrated in William Rubin, *Anthony Caro* (New York, Museum of Modern Art, 1975), pp. 96–97.

processes, rather than from the viewer upward to the transcendental infinite.

David Smith is in many ways the great exemplar of the modern artist in America. Coming from provincial and puritanical roots, he mastered European art —probably with greater thoroughness than any of his contemporaries—without losing his identity and his relation to his own culture. He worked ceaselessly, with tremendous self-discipline, and often in isolation, as sculptor, draftsman, painter, poet. He was possessed by a true ambition, focused on reaching the highest realization of his art rather than on the uncertainties of public acclaim, valuing freedom and integrity above all else. It is inconceivable that he did not have full awareness of his goals and the difficulties they presented. That he succeeded brilliantly is beyond dispute; but what remains an open question is whether his achievements, along with those of his Abstract Expressionist contemporaries, were a unique and privileged event in modern culture or were instead the beginning of a new tradition that has yet to see its finest hour. It is the uncertain outcome of this promise and challenge that now envelops Smith's works with an ever-growing poignancy, inextricably mingled with their grandeur.

David Smith
Painter, Sculptor, Draftsman

Miranda McClintic

David Smith is generally considered one of America's greatest artists, yet there has been no comprehensive study of the full extent of his oeuvre. This exhibition presents for the first time outside of Smith's studios at Bolton Landing a retrospective selection of all the media in which he worked. Paintings, drawings, and sculpture — as well as a variety of works in other media — were interdependent parts of his single, most exceptional vision. Smith considered them all "segments of [his] work life," saying: "If you prefer one work over another, it is your privilege, but it does not interest me. The work is a statement of identity, it comes from a stream, it is related to my past works, the three or four works in process and the work yet to come." [1]

Mastery of all media and disregard of distinctions separating one genre from another were central to this prolific artist's ambition. This approach was influenced by his long study of the art of past times and many cultures. Smith visited museums and galleries regularly and read art books and magazines voraciously. Judging from notations in his sketchbooks and from his extensive library, his interests ranged from primitive art to Japanese calligraphy, from cave painting to Hieronymus Bosch. He believed that an artist had to be sophisticated in his understanding of the history of art but had to work "with the innocence that art never existed before he existed." [2] Smith saw himself as "a discoverer . . . dealing with the projection beyond the known toward a vulgarity" rather than a "functionary dealing with variants of known beauties." [3] From his study of art history, he determined that extensive production in several media was a necessary condition for greatness. With almost moral conviction, David Smith produced an extraordinary amount of work during his thirty-five year career: paintings, sculptures, drawings, etchings, lithographs, jewelry, ceramics, photographs, fireplace tools, his house and studios at Bolton Landing, sculptural towers that carried electricity onto his property, and his father's tombstone. He created along with this, in his voluminous writings and photographs, a record of how he saw his art.

Smith's carefully considered ambition was fostered by a need to work conditioned by the Protestant work ethic and by his relative isolation during much of his life. This promoted a high degree of self-identification with his work, which is evident in the questions he addressed to his students: "Do you make art your life, that which always comes first and occupies every moment, the last problem before sleep and the first awaking vision? Do all the things you like or do amplify and enjoin the progress of art vision and art making?" [4] Although he cared deeply for his family and friends and was often lonely without them, he separated himself from people, both deliberately and unconsciously, for the sake of his art. "Work has always given me back more than anyone or anything," he once said. [5] Smith had a compulsion to make something out of everything he saw around him, and he had great self-discipline. "I maintain my identity by regular work," he declared. "There is always labor when inspiration has fled, but inspiration returns quicker when identity and the work stream is maintained." [6] He worked through ideas over and over again — whether they were images from reality or more abstract configurations — in the same, almost obsessive way he collected and reformed found objects and raw materials.

Smith believed that artists have to "have the courage to try anything. Refuse to be bound down by what others have done or might think. There is progress when artists dare to break with tradition and bring to art whatever innovations their creative genius might offer." [7] Thus, he enthusiastically worked with any material that came his way — whether a rusted found object or the finest paper, silver, or steel — and worked with it according to the

1. McCoy, *David Smith*, p. 84.

2. Ibid., p. 177.

3. David Smith Papers, roll N.D.D., frame 0003.

4. McCoy, *David Smith*, p. 111.

5. Ibid., p. 149.

6. David Smith Papers, roll N.D.4, frame 0500.

7. David Smith in Forbes Watson, "From Studio to Forge," *American Artist*, March 1940, p. 31.

Figure 1 *Steel Drawing*, c. 1945, pen and ink on paper, 25.4 x 18 cm (10 x 7⅛ inches). Candida and Rebecca Smith, New York

Figure 2 *Drawing for Willard Gallery Poster*, 1953, pencil, watercolor, and gouache on paper, 66.5 x 50.5 cm (26³⁄₁₆ x 19⅞ inches). Candida and Rebecca Smith, New York

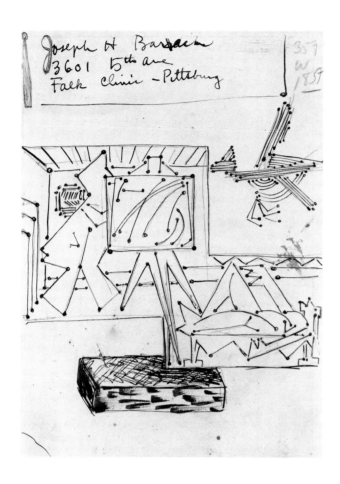

sculpture because of the momentum he sustained by constantly working in two dimensions. Having discovered that sculpture "can come from the found discards in nature, from sticks and stones and parts and pieces, assembled or monolithic, solid form, open form, lines of form, or, like a painting, the illusion of form," [9] Smith proceeded to make all these different kinds of sculpture. Although he incorporated coral, bones, and frying pans in constructions, most of the found objects he used came from the worlds of industry and agriculture — two areas of life with which he strongly identifed. He used wood, bronze, steel, aluminum, silver, and stainless steel alone and often in surprising combinations. His sculpture took the forms of planar collage, linear diagrams in space, volumetric structures, and assemblages of found objects or prefabricated geometric shapes. Many of his sculptures were colored with paint, vitreous enamel, chemicals, molten metals, or with the reflected colors of nature.

Smith saw himself included among the greatest artists of all time, measured his work against theirs, and adapted their accomplishments to his own art. His study of Dutch and Flemish artists of the fifteenth century convinced him of the importance of drawing, and his meticulous draftsmanship may owe something to their example. He learned the craft and technique of etching from the work of Goya. He aimed for the unity between painting and sculpture that he found in primitive art, as well as its eidetic image and intrinsic monumentality. His medallions were inspired by Sumerian seals, his wheeled sculpture by Giacometti. The power of expressive gesture he observed in Japanese painting — particularly the "beginning of a stroke outside the paper continuing through the drawing space to project beyond, so that the included part possesses both the power of origin and projection" [10] — accorded with and perhaps influenced the direct expressiveness of his work. He found in Japanese painting "a natural quality not to be reworked," revealing the means and process of execution, "the nervous current" that transmits the artist's feelings about a subject into its representation. [11]

needs of his vision rather than according to customary usage. Smith made photographs from collaged and inscribed negatives, painted his stainless steel sculptures, and was the first artist known to use spray paint on canvas. Always eager to try something new, he made paintings that ranged from pure geometric abstractions, to surrealist fantasies, to depictions of sculpture, to expressionistic nudes. Smith's drawings were "studies for sculpture, sometimes what sculpture is, sometimes what sculpture can never be." [8] Economy of line and precise description were characteristic of both preparatory sketches for sculpture (fig. 1) and portraits of completed sculptures (fig. 2). Smith created lyrically beautiful drawings that are painterly in their imagery and application of color and was able to transfer the speed and agility that went into making his more expressionistic drawings, like *Timeless Clock* (fig. 3), into

8. Gray, *David Smith by David Smith*, p. 104.

9. McCoy, *David Smith*, p. 147.

10. Ibid., p. 83.

11. Ibid.

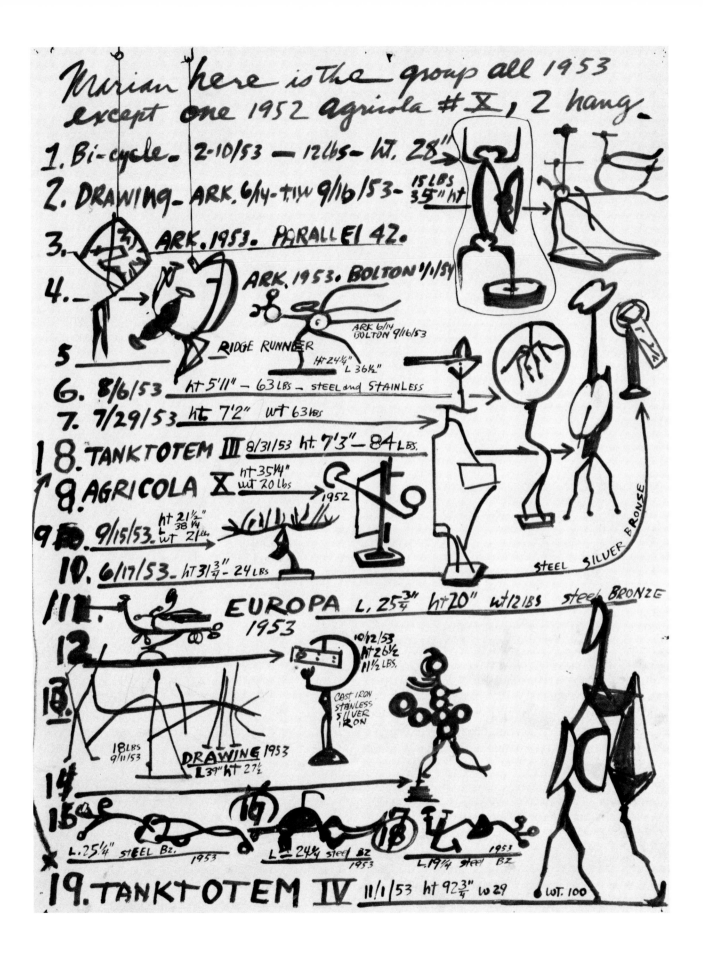

Marian here is the group all 1953 except one 1952 agricola # X, 2 hang.

1. Bi-cycle - 2-10/53 — 12 lbs - ht. 28"

2. DRAWING- ARK. 6/14 - thu 9/16/53 - 15 LBS 3.5" ht

3. ARK. 1953. PARALLEL 42.

4.

ARK. 1953. BOLTON 9/1/54

RIDGE RUNNER

ARK 6/14 BOLTON 9/16/53
Ht 24¼" L 36½"

5.

6. 8/6/53 ht 5'11" — 63 LBS - STEEL and STAINLESS

7. 7/29/53 ht 7'2" wt 63 lbs

8. TANKTOTEM III 8/31/53 ht. 7'3" — 84 LBS.

8. AGRICOLA X ht 35¼" wt 20 lbs

1952

9. 9/15/53. ht 21½" 38¼" L wt 21 lbs

10. 6/17/53 - ht 31¾" - 24 LBS

STEEL SILVER BRONSE

11. EUROPA L, 25¾" ht 20" wt 12 LBS steel BRONZE

1953

12. 10/12/53 ht 26½" 11½ LBS.

CAST IRON STAINLESS SILVER IRON

13. 18 LBS 9/11/53 DRAWING 1953 L 39" ht 27½

14.

15. L. 25¼" STEEL Bz. 1953   L. 24¼ steel Bz 1953   L. 19¼ steel Bz 1953

19. TANKTOTEM IV 11/1/53 ht 92¾" w 29 wt. 100

Figure 3 *Timeless Clock,* 1957, watercolor on paper,
51.3 x 66.7 cm (20³⁄₁₆ x 26¼ inches).
Candida and Rebecca Smith, New York

Among his contemporaries, Smith regarded Picasso as both an example and a rival. When David Smith and Dorothy Dehner were in Paris in 1935, John Graham offered to introduce them to Picasso. Smith, then thirty and unproven as an artist, declined the privilege because he had been told that Picasso expected to be called "maître" and the young American would not acknowledge this supremacy.[12] From then on, the many references Smith made to Picasso in his letters, speeches, and notebook soliloquies indicate how much Smith thought about Picasso. There are also indications in Smith's works that he regularly looked over his shoulder at Picasso, particularly in his cubist and surrealist paintings of the 1930s, in the

12. Wilken, *David Smith,* pp. 9–10.

Medals for Dishonor (plate 8), in *Reclining Figure* (plate 16) and *Steel Drawing* (plate 57), in the bronze casting of found objects to make large sculpture, and in his ceramics (plate 18). Most profoundly, Picasso inspired Smith's overall multimedia proliferation. Echoes of the work of other contemporaries testify to his ambition to take from the greatest art and do it one better. Like Calder, he made a mobile (plate 70) but discovered he preferred the illusion of suggested movement to the real thing. He paralleled the manner of Jackson Pollock in painted bone reliefs (plate 68) and in poured paintings of nudes (plate 17). There are similarities to de Kooning in drawings (plate 56) and in a gestural sculpture (plate 45) with pink, green, and yellow applied in rugged, expressionist brushwork.

Franz Kline's influence is evident in such drawings as an untitled abstraction (plate 58).

Smith incorporated diverse aspects of both Western and Eastern art into his work while reforming the images and objects of his own world. He distinguished himself by using materials and techniques particular to his time, but he also worked expertly in oil, watercolor, and bronze. His constructions of found objects and tools were as exquisite as those he molded in silver. He represented subjects and themes that have long been traditional in art — the figure, landscape, still life, interiors, and animals — but did so in terms that revealed his personal ways of seeing and making. From the first, his richly associative art depended on the impetus and information provided by working simultaneously in a variety of styles and media.

The inventive variety of Smith's production is as impressive at the beginning of his career as at its conclusion. His work in the thirties consists of paintings, drawings, sculpture, photographs of sculpture, photographs made from collaged and inscribed negatives, photographs of still-life arrangements, several painted reliefs, a series of relief medallions, two collages, and several etchings. The paintings include naturalistic depictions of Bolton Landing and the Virgin Islands, abstractly patterned landscapes, stylized urban scenes, and surreal dreamscapes; figures variously influenced by cubism, primitive art, and surrealism; synthetic cubist still lifes and studio interiors; studies for sculpture and portraits of sculpture. Although each painting is unmistakably his own, traces of ideas from Jan Matulka, John Graham, Stuart Davis, Joan Miró, André Masson, Georges Braque, and Paul Klee are evident. Many of these works are similar to those of the American Abstract Artists in having a one to one correspondence between real and abstract form and an overall linear network, which is colored in to differentiate one plane from another. Colors range from bold primaries to sturdy earth tones to acidic pastels. Smith's drawings of the 1930s are more limited in subject and composition than his paintings. Among them are academic and cubist nudes, still-life images of shells and coral interlayered with maplike landscapes of the Virgin Islands, surreal bone figures, realistic and abstract dancers, studies related to

paintings, and literal sketches for sculpture. Drawings were frequently related to sculptures, but there is little connection between Smith's drawings and paintings in this decade. He seldom used color across an entire sheet, and never as a major compositional element; occasionally forms are touched with color or color is used as a halo to silhouette sculptural shapes. Having had no formal sculptural training, Smith was pleased to discover from the example of Picasso and González that sculpture could be made from anything. He moved freely from the coral used for his first sculpture to wood, iron, steel, and bronze — learning to carve, forge, weld, cast, and assemble as he went along. These early works ranged from linear diagrams to volumetric structures to realistic torsos. Organic shapes were as common as geometric; curved lines as frequent as straight. Many works depended on cubist alternation of line and plane; others utilized surrealist biomorphism or expressive gesture.

In the early forties, Smith's output decreased considerably because of his wartime job in Schenectady and because he built his own house and studio during those years. Yet he made jewelry and etchings at the start of the decade, and after 1945 made paintings, drawings, sculpture, and photographs in substantial numbers. Surreal images of metamorphosis, violence, and entrapment were prevalent in Smith's work in the forties. Biomorphic forms, dramatic compositions, and fantastic colors were used to express states of mind that were personal in intensity but universal in resonance. Some of his most lyrical works (dancers, musicians, landscapes) are in this decade as well as his most frightening. The paintings and drawings are largely figurative. Several paintings and most drawings relate closely to specific sculptures. In sculpture, figures, interiors, landscapes, and birds are the principle subjects. Smith worked in cast aluminum, marble, stainless steel, silver, and nickel in addition to the materials he used previously. The forms of these sculptures are more substantial and they are inherently more monumental than those of the thirties.

The fifties was the most inventive and productive decade of Smith's career. He made paintings in oil, Magna, and metallic spray paint; cardboard collages; painted reliefs; drawings in innumerable styles and media; his most linear sculpture and his most volumetric; sculptural reliefs in silver as well as bronze; lithographs; etchings; photographs of sculpture and aerial photographs of landscape; and jewelry. His paintings included landscapes vibrating with expressionist brushwork; figures and interiors defined by a cubist network of lines and planes; pictures of totemic sculptures; and spray paintings that began with sculptural images and became increasingly pictorial. Some drawings of the 1950s were related to sculpture, but these are more highly finished and evocative than in previous decades. Many others are purely calligraphic, and many are painterly. There was great diversity in the sculpture, which included linear constructions of agricultural tools and equipment, linear steel drawings in space, humorous figures made from found objects cast in bronze, kitsch Abstract Expressionist molten bronze pieces, collages of overlapping planes of steel, planar silhouettes, and pillars of stainless steel boxes. For the first time, much of Smith's sculpture was large in size as well as scale, but the smaller works of this period are equally powerful.

In the sixties, Smith's work in all media became increasingly expansive. He was not only fully in command of his powers, and an acknowledged master to an ever-widening group of admirers, but he was at last able to afford large stocks of materials and the help of assistants. He forged new territory with his nudes as well as with his spray paintings, which were unique in relation to painting being done by other artists at the time. The expressive boldness of the poured enamel in the nudes was as carefully controlled as the modulated layers of spray paint. The forms in the spray paintings are (as in his sculpture of the 1960s) fewer in number and stronger in definition, as demonstrated by *Cubi XIX* of 1964 (fig. 4 and plate 112). His drawings demonstrate precision as well as imagination. His images acquired an even greater freedom from static sculptural form, and he worked in an astonishingly diverse selection of media. He made ceramic plates (plate 18) and plaques, and continued to take thousands of photographs documenting his life and work. In the last years of his life, Smith made the most daringly ethereal and most solidly tangible sculptures of his career. He colored some of his sculpture with neo-expressionist brushwork, others

with solid, "gutty" [13] colors or lively push-pull complementaries; and still others were colored by the world around them as reflected in stainless steel.

Virtuosity as well as persistent productivity distinguish David Smith's manner of working. His oeuvre is characterized by a multiplicity of styles that he practiced concurrently — each having its own imperatives, challenges, and accomplishments. His styles were never pure. Geometric abstraction, organic abstraction, surrealist puns, expressionism, voluminosity, linearity, violence, or humor might be the predominant feature in a given group of works, but other, usually contrasting, elements were always present. Overlapping and amalgamation of styles dated from the simultaneous influences that first informed his art in the thirties: figurative and synthetic cubism, surrealism, constructivism, expressionism, social realism, and primitive art. Distinctions had not been made between Kandinsky, Picasso, Matisse, Miró, Mondrian, Léger, and Klee. Style as such, never a relevant consideration for Smith, had little to do with the continuity in his work, or with its variety.

Smith moved as freely from one medium to another as he did among various styles. "The one rule," he declared, "is that there may be no rules." [14] It was not common among Smith's American contemporaries for an artist to work so extensively in as many media as he did, but it was a given assumption in Europe. Smith followed the example of Picasso, Matisse, González, and Giacometti (among others) in defining himself broadly as an artist. Although he considered sculpture his principal means of expression, he painted and drew constantly and produced as many paintings and drawings as did artists who worked exclusively in those media. His work in each of his chosen media had its own particular character and followed its own internal development, dictated as much by the properties of different materials as by Smith's determination to expand the limits of media. Nonetheless, there are distinctive qualities of temperament and craft common to all of Smith's work, which are crucial to our understanding of it.

Repeatedly described by those who knew him as a

13. Gray, *David Smith by David Smith*, p. 124.
14. McCoy, *David Smith*, p. 183.

Figure 4 *Cubi XIX*, 1964, stainless steel,
287.3 x 55.2 x 52.7 cm (113⅛ x 21¾ x 20¾ inches).
Tate Gallery, London

person of enormous energy, David Smith transmitted that energy to his art. This extension of his personality was something he valued in his work. "If the vitality is there," he said, "the shape will grow form. The quality of vitality I feel comes first—other orders follow." [15] Always based on a concentration of natural form and space to abstract line and plane, Smith's works are remarkable in the decisive clarity of their images, and in the richness of expression and association that is concentrated within a concisely articulated structure. Sharpness of linear contour or planar silhouette, asymmetrical balance, a sense of just proportion, and sophisticated manipulation of space keep these images in the mind's eye long after they have been seen. Smith's art gains much of its character and strength from its surprising combinations of forms, colors, scales, and surfaces into what he described as a "unity that did not exist before." [16] Underlying these combinations is a tension that comes from the assumption and incorporation of characteristics generally considered as opposites. Such qualities are not synthesized in Smith's work, any more than they were resolved in his personality: conflicting impulses and assertions, fully expressed, are simultaneously present in both. David Smith saw himself as an industrial laborer, an outdoor man, and a farmer, and equally as a maker and connoisseur of art, a sophisticated gourmet, and a lover of fine music. Boundless generosity could be matched with relentless selfishness (generally for the sake of his art) and gentleness alternated with macho volatility. Paralleling this in the work is the coincidence of intractable materials and poetic temperament, industrial technique and natural gesture, brute strength and gentle wit, awkwardness and lyricism, geometric form and organic form. The most fundamental duality in Smith's art is its assumption of the premises and potentials of both abstraction and realism. Smith combined essentualizing reduction of form and schematic compositional designs with images, themes, and materials that associatively related to reality. In this, Smith's art belongs to the first half of the twentieth century. Like Picasso, Matisse, González, Brancusi, and Giacometti, whose works he

most admired, Smith never embraced pure non-objectivity. "There is no such thing as *truly* abstract," he said. "Man always has to work from his life." [17]

There are particular qualities of craft that are common to all of Smith's works, irrespective of media. The concentrated attention and technical ingenuity with which he approached everything he did is evident in his art. With obsessive persistence, he worked through enormous stocks of materials, just as he worked through numerous permutations of an idea, or through a particular stylistic mode until he exhausted it. Thus, it was as characteristic for him to produce works using boiler caps (*Tanktotem* series) or rectangular boxes and cubes (*Cubi* series), as to make more than thirty paintings, drawings, and sculptures on the billiard player theme between 1935 and 1946, or to execute hundreds of purely calligraphic drawings in the 1950s. David Smith wanted to try everything and was determined to do everything well, whether it was to prepare a meal or to weld a ten-foot sculpture.

Fine craftsmanship was important to Smith. He was introduced to fundamental paint techniques in the early thirties by reading Max Doerner's *The Materials of the Artist* and through working with Ralph Mayer on WPA mural projects. Smith also did his own research and practical experimentation with a wide range of traditional and non-traditional materials. He habitually made notes on the condition of works he saw in museums and kept records of his own experiments on the backs of his paintings and in his notebooks. He wrote and lectured on chemical formulas, the properties of particular materials, and the potential applications of specific techniques. He never hesitated to spend money for the best materials: specially ground colors for paintings, imported papers for drawings, even silver for sculptures (plates 75, 87). When he traveled to Greece in 1935–36, he scraped minute paint samples from ancient columns so as to learn the secret of color stability and longevity by means of microscopic examination. Still working on the same problem in the 1960s, he discovered that nothing was better for painting his sculptures than automobile enamel, which he applied in twenty-five or thirty coats, three times the number used on a

15. David Smith Papers, roll N.D.4, frame 0968.

16. McCoy, *David Smith*, p. 39.

17. Ibid., p. 171.

Mercedes.[18] The precision and extent of his welding far surpassed the dictates of purely structural considerations: as with all his methods and techniques, it was a matter of pride in craftmanship. Smith freely combined contemporary materials and technologies with traditional ones. These combinations were usually straightforward, such as the use within a single sculpture of cast bronze, welded steel, forged iron, and molten copper. On canvas, he combined traditional brushstrokes with spray painting. In other cases, the processes were more complex, such as in the steel plate etchings he made in the fifties, where "abstract forms are sawed out of steel plate, then etched, engraved, hammered, chiseled, etc. . . . the individual parts then welded to a bed plate before printing."[19]

To Smith it was important not only to have quality materials, tools, and equipment, but also to have quantity. "One thing I learned from working in factories," he said, "is that people who make things — whether it's automobiles, ships or locomotives — have to have a plentiful supply of materials . . . . Art can't be made by a poor mouth, and I have to forget the cost problem because it's always more than I can afford."[20] He stocked and worked regularly in bronze, stainless steel, cold and hot rolled steel, copper, cast iron, aluminum, found objects and tools, oil paint, gouache, automobile enamel, canned spray paint, Magna, watercolors, waxes, and lacquers. Rolls of canvas and reams of paper were always on hand. Buying material by the truckload was a matter of both expediency and inspiration. Not only did he feel "that the aesthetic vision [should not be] limited by material need,"[21] he also believed that with time a material becomes "personal and fits into visionary use. With possession and acquaintance, a fluidity developed which was not there."[22]

The resolute conviction of Smith's vision ensured the extraordinary continuity in his art, whereas his empathetic response to materials and their potential was responsible for the variety found in his work. Characteristically, he would focus at any given time almost exclusively on one particular material, a type of found object, or an abstract shape, and work it through as many permutations and combinations as he could invent. His career can be seen as a sequence of infatuations, often simultaneous, with chosen materials, found objects, or particular abstract shapes such as the circles and cubes that were prefabricated for him. Working with such a wide range of materials and component parts appealed to the technical ingenuity that Smith had developed as a child in Decatur, Indiana, following his father's example. A variety of ever-new approaches and solutions continually expanded the boundaries of his art. This experimentation was paralleled by the repeated restatement, with ever greater resonance, of favorite themes and formal configurations — the images that Smith carried around in his mind's eye throughout his life. Projected into his art, they were consistently reworked in the same way that he rewrote his thoughts in notebook ruminations, formal lectures, and letters to friends until he expressed countless nuances and ramifications of the ideas that were most important to him. Such repetition using different modes of representation recalls Cézanne's involvement with apples and Mont Sainte-Victoire, which Smith discussed at length in his writings. Both artists were involved with empathetic response, with isolating the elemental structural bases of reality, and with the suggestive power of familiar images.

Some of Smith's chosen themes — such as the figure and landscape — represent a lifetime involvement, while others were limited to discrete periods of time. Each subject is treated variously as to medium, style, degree of abstraction, and emotional tone, but all manifestations are linked by a fundamental approach. The figure — reclining, moving, standing — is the most important theme in Smith's paintings, drawings, and sculpture. Ranging from directly observed and realistic to schematically or skeletally abstract, each figure has distinct qualities of personality as well as anatomy. Most are female in allusion and give view to the full range of Smith's feelings toward women, but in the 1950s a number of male figures — totems and sentinels — appear in all media. Reclining figures were common in Smith's sculpture

18. Gray, *David Smith by David Smith*, p. 118.

19. McCoy, *David Smith*, p. 69.

20. Elaine de Kooning, "David Smith Makes a Sculpture," *Art News* 50 (September 1951): 39.

21. Gray, *David Smith by David Smith*, p. 55.

22. David Smith Papers, roll N.D.3, frame 1339.

Figure 5 *Untitled* (reclining nude), 1953, ink on paper, 74 x 106 cm, sight (29 x 41¾ inches, sight). Fogg Art Museum, Harvard University, gift of Mrs. Culver Orswell (1974.155)

Figure 6 *Cubi XXVI*, 1965, stainless steel, 303.4 x 383.4 x 65.6 cm (119½ x 151 x 25⅞ inches). National Gallery of Art, Washington, D.C., Ailsa Mellon Bruce Fund, 1978

1936 (plate 7); *Untitled* (bony dancers), 1937 (plate 50); the *Medal for Dishonor: Munitions Makers*, 1939 (plate 8); the drawing related to *Munitions Makers*, 1940 (plate 9); *Untitled* (two bony figures), 1946 (plate 36); *Royal Bird*, 1948 (plate 82); *Chicken Bones*, 1951 (plate 79); *Yellow Vertical*, 1955 (plate 105); *Untitled* (standing woman), 1956 (plate 103); and *Untitled* (skeletal network), c. 1958 (plate 104).

Much of the vitality of Smith's work comes from his replication of the functioning of natural forces such as movement, resistance, tension, balance, and growth. One or another of these forces, or several together are present in most of Smith's works. He found countless ways of representing them, among which the most

common are: upward gestural extensions of line or plane; compositions that are asymmetrically or precariously balanced; tenuous points of connection between forms; and the free-floating suspension of form in space, defying the limitations of gravity.

From his earliest constructions until the stainless steel monuments at the end of his career, David Smith's sculpture reflected the compositional principles that characterize his paintings and drawings. He was always involved with the concentration of natural form and space to abstract line and plane, the play of similar negative and positive shapes, and implied movement. Smith arranged plane, color, and gesture non-referentially and non-descriptively in

Figure 10 *Untitled,* 1937–40, collage with pen and ink, gouache, 27.9 x 21.7 cm (11 x 8½ inches). Candida and Rebecca Smith, New York

Figure 11 *Fifteen Planes,* 1958, stainless steel, 290.5 x 151.1 x 41.2 cm (114⅜ x 59½ x 16¼ inches). University of Seattle

space as easily as on canvas or paper. Because image took precedence over structure, the placement of forms was more important than shaping them three-dimensionally.

Linear contour and planar silhouette were fundamental to Smith's art. Derived from the cubist network of line and plane, linear contour provided a "comment as mass and space more acute than bulk shape."[24] Like planar silhouette, it allowed for the precise definition of image that was one of the great strengths of Smith's works in all media.

Collage was another compositional principle that was always central to Smith's work. Although his first known collage (fig. 10) dates from the late thirties, he used its methods in his early reliefs (plate 5). He applied the additive method of construction to most of his sculpture, but it was only in the 1950s that collagelike overlapping of planes became important in both painting and sculpture. In 1957, Smith made several cardboard collage studies (plate 88) for his

sculptures (fig. 11), and in the next year began to make spray paintings that were in fact negative collages. At the same time, Smith began building his sculpture by layering one plane or object in front of another, a practice that he continued for the rest of his life (plates 26, 30, 59, 108, 111, 115, 116).

David Smith's vision was that of a painter or draftsman. He sought to present images and express states of mind, emotion, and perception that traditionally belong within the province of painting and drawing. Yet, he felt most comfortable with the processes and materials of industrially based sculpture, and he identified himself with workingmen.[25] Smith declared, "The work flow of energy demanded by sculpture wherein mental exhaustion is accompanied by physical exhaustion, provides the only balance I've ever found, and as far as I know is the only way of life."[26] Nonetheless, Smith believed above all that "sculpture is a conceptual process,"[27] and that the artist should not be a conceptual slave to material.[28] He said, "I make no separate division for the cause of sculpture from painting. The preference governing actual material is personal. The material use of a dimension instead of an indicated dimension changes no method of conception. The concept in either craft comes from the expression of emotion and thought. The difference in technical pursuit does not change the mind's reaction to form."[29]

By working in various media, Smith maintained a steady transformation of inspiration into expression, which gave exceptional immediacy and intensity to all his work. All of David Smith's explorations reflected his belief that "the artist must work towards that which he does not know. Whether this is called invention or finding or searching, it must be a projection beyond the given state of art."[30] In the exceptional richness and variety of his work, we find the rewards of this approach.

24. David Smith Papers, roll N.D.4, frame 1094.

25. "By choice I identify myself with working men and still belong to Local 2054 United Steelworkers of America. I belong by craft — yet the subject of aesthetics introduces a breach" (McCoy, *David Smith,* p. 22).

26. Gray, *David Smith by David Smith,* p. 39.

27. Ibid., p. 58.

28. David Smith Papers, roll N.D.5, frame 0082.

29. Ibid., roll N.D.4, frame 1061.

30. Gray, *David Smith by David Smith,* p. 134.

Chronology

1906

March 9, David Roland Smith born to Golda Stoler and Harvey Martin Smith in Decatur, Indiana. Father was a telephone engineer and part-time inventor; mother was a schoolteacher.

1911

April 7, sister Katherine born in Decatur (now Mrs. Forrest A. Stewart of Fort Myers, Fla.).

1921

Moves with family to Paulding, Ohio, where father becomes manager and part-owner of Paulding Telephone Company. Attends Paulding High School.

1923

Takes correspondence course in drawing from Cleveland Art School. Official artist for Paulding High School yearbook.

1924

Spring, graduates from high school. Fall, enters Ohio University, Athens, for one year; studies woodcut, but finds that most courses prepare students to be art teachers rather than artists.

1925

Summer, works in South Bend, Indiana, as a welder and riveter at Studebaker plant; also sells bonds. Fall, enters Notre Dame University, South Bend, for one semester.

1926

Early in the year moves to Washington, D.C. Works for Morris Plan Bank. Summer, attends two poetry classes at George Washington University (disliked nineteenth-century Romantic poetry). Moves to New York City to pursue a career as an artist. Fall, meets Dorothy Dehner (through Mrs. Haberton, their mutual landlady at 417 West 118th Street), who tells him about the Art Students League. Enrolls at the League and studies evenings with Richard Lahey. Works for Industrial Acceptance Corporation, whose offices on West 57th Street were close to the League. Meets the painter Edgar Levy.

1927

Spring, continues studying with Lahey at the League. Fall, becomes full-time student at Art Students League (until 1932), studying painting with Lahey and John Sloan. Makes prints at night and on Saturdays. December 24, marries Dorothy Dehner at City Hall, New York City. Moves to 15 Abingdon Square in Greenwich Village.

1928

Studies drawing with Kimon Nicolaides at the League. With Dehner, makes posters advertising Birch Elixir for Theosophical Society. Does illustrations for *The Sportsman Pilot* (until 1931). Works as self-titled "Director of Accommodations" for the sporting goods store A. G. Spalding, doing design and display. Summer, visits Dehner's family in California. Fall, moves to two-room apartment in Brooklyn on Myra Court (name later changed to Beekman Place), Flatbush. Becomes friendly with the painters Thomas and Weber Furlong, with whom he visits Bolton Landing on Lake George in upstate New York.

1929

Summer, goes to Bolton Landing for a month as paying guest of the Furlongs. Buys Old Fox Farm in Bolton Landing, which he visits on weekends while continuing to live in Brooklyn. Meets John Graham through the Furlongs. Fall, moves to 163 Sterling Street, Flatbush. For entire year studies with Jan Matulka, who introduces him to European modernism. (Dorothy Dehner, Lucille Corcos, Francis Criss, Burgoyne Diller, Al Kramer, Bella Kroll, Edgar Levy, Mary Lorence, George McNeil, Irene Rice Pereira, and Jim Robertson are in the same class.)

1930

Studies with Matulka at the League. Introduced by Graham to Milton Avery, David Burliuk, Stuart Davis, Arshile Gorky, Frederick Kiesler, and Jean Xceron. Occasionally (until 1931) does layouts for *Tennis*, magazine of United States Lawn Tennis Association. *Group exhibition:* "4th Annual Exhibition of American Block Prints," Print Club of Philadelphia, March 17–April 5 (Smith's work exhibited for the first time).

1931

June–July, after Matulka's class at the League is canceled, Smith, Dehner, Diller, Lorence, Kramer, McNeil, Pereira, and Robertson set up a studio so they can continue their studies with Matulka privately. Goes to Bolton Landing for part of summer. October, goes to St. Thomas in the Virgin Islands with Dorothy Dehner (until 1932). Paints on canvas and panel and makes first sculptures: a torso and a small head, both carved out of coral and painted.

1932

June or July, returns to New York, bringing back shells, fishbones, and coral that are later incorporated into sculpture. Makes constructions. At Bolton Landing, in a woodshed (to which he added a skylight) behind the house, begins working with a forge (obtained from a defunct blacksmith shop in Ticonderoga). In New York, moves to 124 State Street, Brooklyn Heights. First painting exhibited when Herman Baron displays an abstract landscape, executed in the Virgin Islands, in the window of ACA Gallery, New York. Establishes studio in corner of Terminal Iron Works, Brooklyn, a machine shop where fire escapes for public schools are produced (works there until 1940). Makes first welded steel sculpture, one of *Head* series.

1933

Spring, at Bolton Landing, continues making sculpture from wood, wire, melted lead. Works on series of *Heads,* which may have been first painted welded-steel sculptures made in U.S. Fall, sculpts and welds at Barney Snyder's garage in Bolton Landing. (Inspired by work of Picasso and González.) Returns to New York City and works at Spalding's. Buys welding outfit. Friends with Adolph Gottlieb, Louis Harris, Louis Schanker, Gregorio Prestopino. November (to March 1934), makes bases out of exotic woods for African sculpture John Graham had purchased in Europe for the collection of Frank Crowninshield. *Group exhibition:* Feragil Galleries, New York (exhibits several watercolors executed on blueprint paper).

1934

March, serves as technical assistant (self-taught) for New York mural painting project of Public Works of Art Project, superseded by Temporary Emergency Relief Administration in April. August, becomes assistant project supervisor (until July 1935). Evaluates and recommends procedures and media for post office murals, and teaches techniques to artists working on murals. Given a González sculpture by Graham. *Group exhibition:* "Winter Exhibition of Paintings," Academy of Allied Arts, New York, January 18–February 10.

1935

Becomes a member, with Gorky, Graham, de Kooning, Levy, and Mischa Resnikoff, of group that notifies Whitney Museum of American Art, New York, that they would exhibit in "Abstract Art in America" only if all were invited, which they were not. October, leaves for Europe with Dorothy Dehner; goes first to Paris and Brussels, then to Greece at the end of November. Paints throughout trip. Makes a bronze in Greece, then destroys it because the casting is bad.

1936

In Greece and Crete, then returns to France via Malta. In Paris, paints and makes several etchings while spending several weeks at Stanley William Hayter's Atelier 17. Visits London and USSR. July 4, returns to U. S. Spends remainder of summer at Bolton Landing. Makes first modeled wax pieces for bronze castings. Works on oxyacetylene-welded sculpture. Makes *Reclining Figure.* Late fall, returns to New York and Terminal Iron Works. Lives at 57 Poplar Street, Brooklyn.

1937

February, assigned to Works Project Administration to work as a sculptor (until August 1939). Begins first of fifteen *Medals for Dishonor,* using dentists' and jewelers' tools. Marian Willard, East River Gallery, agrees to give him a solo exhibition during following year. (Willard remains his dealer until 1956.) Summer at Bolton Landing. Meets Jackson Pollock.

1938

Keeps working at Terminal Iron Works. Spends summer at Bolton Landing and does lost-wax bronzes. *Solo exhibition:* "David Smith Steel Sculpture," East River Gallery, New York, January 19–February 5 (first solo exhibition; 17 welded-iron sculptures and a number of drawings shown). *Group exhibition:* Second Annual Membership Exhibition, American Artists' Congress, New York.

1939

First arc-welded sculpture. Commissioned by Museum of Modern Art, New York, to make fireplace tools and andirons for museum's penthouse. August 4, father dies; makes bronze plaque for headstone. *Group exhibitions:* "American Abstract Artists," Riverside Museum, New York, March 7–26; "Exhibition of Contemporary American Art," New York World's Fair, April–October.

1940

Spring, Smiths move to Bolton Landing permanently; names studio Terminal Iron Works. George L. K. Morris buys *Bi-Polar Structure* (1937). Lectures on "Abstract Art in America" with Stuart Davis and Irene Rice Pereira at United American Artists Local 60, New York. Works as a machinist in nearby Glens Falls. *Solo exhibitions:* "David Smith," J. B. Neumann and Willard Galleries, New York, March 25–April 15; "Medals for Dishonor by David Smith," Willard Gallery, New York, November 5–23 (catalog statements by Smith).

1941

Begins building and equipping studio-workshop at Bolton Landing. *Solo exhibitions:* "Medals for Dishonor," Kalamazoo (Mich.) Institute of Art, February; "Medals for Dishonor," Walker Art Center, Minneapolis, November–December. *Group exhibitions:* "Annual Exhibition of Sculpture, Watercolors, Drawings and Prints," Whitney Museum of American Art, New York, January 15–February 19 (included in every Whitney Annual thereafter except 1957, 1961, 1963, 1965); "Third Outdoor Sculpture Exhibition," Sculptors' Guild, New York, April–May; "Anti-War Show," Congress of American Artists, Hotel Com-

modore, New York, June 6–7; "15 American Sculptors," circulated by Museum of Modern Art, New York, to eleven cities in U.S., 1941–43; "20th-Century Sculpture and Constructions," circulated by Museum of Modern Art, New York, to six cities in U.S., 1941–43.

1942

Works (until 1944) welding tanks on the graveyard shift (midnight to 8:00 a.m.) at American Locomotive Company, Schenectady, N.Y. Lives in three-room attic at 1113 McClellan Street, in Schenectady, and commutes to Bolton Landing on weekends. Draws on weekdays and learns to work with marble while employed half-days at Saratoga (N.Y.) Funeral Monument Yard, Harrison and Mallory Marbleworks. Works on series of black-and-white drawings, including *Italian Theme,* an indictment of Mussolini's fascism. *Solo exhibitions:* "Jewelry by David Smith," Willard Gallery, New York, January; Skidmore College, Saratoga Springs, N.Y., January 10–28. *Group exhibition:* "Artists for Victory," Metropolitan Museum of Art, New York, December 7–February 22.

1943

Museum of Modern Art, New York, acquires *Head* (1938). *Solo exhibition:* "David Smith Sculpture and Drawings (1939–1943)," Willard Gallery, New York, April 6–May 1. *Group exhibition:* "American Sculpture of Our Time," Willard and Buchholz Galleries, New York, January (Smith's *Interior* receives favorable notice from critic Clement Greenberg in *The Nation*).

1944

Leaves Schenectady and returns to live permanently at Bolton Landing. Finishes studio workshop at Bolton Landing; living quarters remain the original farmhouse.

1945

Summer, Dorothy Dehner returns to New York for a short time; Smith works on sculpture and lives alone. *Group exhibition:* "Recent Work by American Sculptors," Buchholz Gallery, New York, February 6–24.

1946

Whitney Museum of American Art purchases *Cockfight Variation* (1945). *Solo exhibitions:* "The Sculpture of David Smith" (retrospective exhibition of 54 sculptures, 1936–45), Willard and Buchholz Galleries, New York, January 2–26; "David Smith," circulated by American Association of University Women to ten cities in U.S., 1946–49.

1947

August, speaks at first Woodstock (N.Y.) Art Conference. *Solo exhibitions:* "Sculpture and Drawings by David Smith," Skidmore College, Saratoga Springs, N.Y., February 4–25; "David Smith Sculpture 1946–1947," Willard Gallery, New York, April 1–26.

1948

First teaching position at Sarah Lawrence College, Bronxville, N.Y. (until 1950). New house at Bolton Landing completed. *Solo exhibition:* "David Smith Medals for Dishonor," Allen R. Hite Art Institute, University of Louisville, Ky., November 29–December 18. *Group exhibition:* "10th Outdoor Sculpture Exhibition," Sculptors' Guild, New York, April.

1949

Designs three prize medals in gold, silver, and bronze for *Art News* National Amateur Painters Competition. *Group exhibition:* "Sculpture," Willard Gallery, New York, January 4–20.

1950

Receives Guggenheim Fellowship for Fine Arts (renewed 1951). Thanksgiving, Dorothy Dehner and Smith separate (divorced 1952). *Solo exhibition:* "David Smith," Willard Gallery, New York, April 18–May 13. *Group exhibitions:* "International Exhibition of Sculpture in the Open Air," Middelheim Park, Antwerp, summer; "Carvers, Modelers, Welders: A Selection of Recent American Sculpture," Museum of Modern Art, New York, August, followed by tour to six cities in U.S., 1952–53.

1951

Lectures at Bennington (Vt.) College, and American University, Washington, D.C. *Solo exhibitions:* "David Smith," Willard Gallery, New York, March 27–April 21; Bennington College, November 16–25. *Group exhibitions:* "Abstract Painting and Sculpture in America," Museum of Modern Art, New York, January 23–March 25; "60th Annual American Exhibition of Paintings and Sculpture," Art Institute of Chicago, October 25–December 16; "American Sculpture 1951," Metropolitan Museum of Art, New York, December 7–February 24; U.S. representation, 1st Bienal, São Paulo, Brazil.

1952

Lectures on WNYC Radio. *Solo exhibitions:* "David Smith Sculpture and Drawings," Willard and Kleemann Galleries, New York, April 1–26; "Sculpture and Drawings—David Smith," Walker Art Center, Minneapolis, April 12–May 11.

1953

Teaches one semester at University of Arkansas, Fayetteville. April 6, marries Jean Freas of Washington, D.C., in Arkansas. May, lectures at Southwestern College Art Conference, University of Oklahoma, Oklahoma City. November, attends American Federation of Arts meeting at Corning Glass Center, Corning, N.Y. *Solo exhibitions:* "David Smith, New Sculpture," Kootz Gallery, New York, January 26–February 14; University of Arkansas, Fayetteville, February; "David Smith Drawings," Willard Gallery, New York, December 15–30. *Group exhibitions:* "Contemporary American Painting and Sculpture," University of Illinois, Urbana, March 1–April 12; Twelve Modern American Painters and Sculptors," circulated by Museum of Modern Art, New York, to six cities in Europe, 1953–54.

1954

April 4, daughter Eve Athena Allen Katherine Rebecca is born. June 18, lectures at Columbia University. August 6, participates in Woodstock Art Conference. Teaches at Indiana University, Bloomington. Visits Europe as delegate to UNESCO's First International Congress of Plastic Arts, Venice. Visits France and Italy. Participates in a symposium at Albright Art Gallery, Buffalo, N.Y. *Solo exhibitions:* "David Smith," Willard Gallery, New York, January 5–30; "David Smith: Sculpture, Drawings, Graphics," Contemporary Arts Center, Cincinnati (Ohio) Art Museum, May 19–June 13, followed by tour to three cities in U.S., 1954. *Group exhibitions:* "2 Painters/3 Sculptors," American Pavilion, 27th Venice Biennale, June–October; "61st American Exhibition of Paintings and Sculpture," Art Institute of Chicago, October 21–December 5.

1955

Teaches at University of Mississippi, Oxford. August 12, second daughter, Candida Kore Nicolina Rawley Hellene, is born.

1956

February, publishes tribute to Julio González in *Art News,* entitled "First Master of the Torch." *Solo exhibition:* "David Smith Sculpture and Drawings, 1954–1956," Willard Gallery, New York, March 6–31. *Group exhibition:* "Exposition Internationale de Sculpture Contemporaine," Musée Rodin, Paris, summer.

1957

Commissioned by Art Institute of Chicago to design Logan Prize medal. *Solo exhibitions:* "David Smith" (retrospective exhibition of sculpture, 1932–57), Museum of Modern Art, New York, September 11–October 20; "Sculpture by David Smith," Fine Arts Associates (Otto Gerson), New York, September 17–October 12; "David Smith: Sculpture in Silver," Widdifield Gallery, New York, October.

1958

Group exhibitions: "Nature in Abstraction," Whitney Museum of American Art, New York, January 14–March 16, followed by tour to six cities in U.S., 1958–59; "Contemporary American Sculpture," United States Pavilion, Brussels World's Fair, April 3–October 30; "Painting-Sculpture: A Decade in Review: England-France-Italy-United States," De Cordova Museum, Lincoln, Mass., April 27–June 1; "Lipton, Rothko, Smith and Tobey," U.S. representation, 29th Venice Biennale, June–October; "1958 Pittsburgh International Exhibition of Contemporary Painting and Sculpture," Department of Fine Arts, Carnegie Institute, December 5–February 8.

1959

Solo exhibitions: "Drawings," New Gallery, Bennington College, March 26; "David Smith Paintings and Drawings," French & Company, New York, September 16–October 10; *Group exhibitions:* "Sculpture in Our Time Collected by Joseph H. Hirshhorn," Detroit Institute of Arts, May 5–August 23, followed by tour to eight cities in U.S. and Canada, 1959–60; "Documenta II: Sculpture," Kassel, West Germany, July 11–October 11; "David Smith: 25 Sculptures," U.S. representation, 5th Bienal, São Paulo, Brazil, September 21–December 31.

1960

February, special issue of *Arts Magazine* devoted to Smith's work, with essay by Hilton Kramer. *Solo exhibitions:* "David Smith Sculpture," French & Company, New York, February–March 19; "Selections: Paintings, Sculpture," Otto Gerson Gallery, New York, summer; "David Smith Sculpture and Drawings," Everett Ellin Gallery, Los Angeles, November 7–December 3.

1961

Refuses third prize at Pittsburgh International, Carnegie Institute (opposed to system of first, second, and third prizes). Divorced from Jean Freas. Becomes affiliated with Otto Gerson Gallery (later the Marlborough-Gerson Gallery), New York. *Solo exhibitions:* "David Smith: Recent Sculpture," Otto Gerson Gallery, New York, October 10–28; "David Smith," Department of Fine Arts, Carnegie Institute, Pittsburgh, Pa., October 27–January 7; "David Smith" (fifty sculptures, 1933–57), circulated by Museum of Modern Art, New York, to nine cities in U.S., 1961–63. *Group exhibition:* "The Art of Assemblage," Museum of Modern Art, New York, October 2–November 20; "Spotlight on Sculpture 1880–1961," Otto Gerson Gallery, New York, December–January.

1962

May–June, participates in Spoleto's Festival of Two Worlds by making 26 sculptures in one month at Voltri, near Genoa. *Group exhibitions:* "Geometric Abstraction in America," Whitney Museum of

American Art, New York, March 20–May 13; "Sculpture in the City," Festival of Two Worlds, Spoleto, Italy, June–July; "Modern Sculpture from the Joseph H. Hirshhorn Collection," Guggenheim Museum, New York, October 3–January 6.

1963
Solo exhibition: "David Smith: A Decade of Drawings 1953–1963," Balin-Traube Gallery, New York, May 14–June 14. *Group exhibitions:* "Sculpture in the Open Air," Battersea Park, London, May–September; "Sculptors of Our Time," Washington Gallery of Modern Art, Washington, D.C., September 17–October 31.

1964
Receives Creative Arts Award from Brandeis University. Program on WNET-TV Art New York series, "David Smith: Welding Master of Bolton Landing," interview with Frank O'Hara. *Solo exhibitions:* "David Smith Sculpture and Drawings," Institute of Contemporary Art, University of Pennsylvania, Philadelphia, February 1–March 15; "David Smith," Marlborough-Gerson Gallery, New York, October. *Group exhibition:* Documenta III, Kassel, West Germany, June–September.

1965
Cubi XXVI, dated January 12, perhaps last completed sculpture. February, appointed by President Lyndon B. Johnson to the National Council on the Arts. May 23, killed in an automobile crash near Bennington, Vermont. May 27, funeral services at Bolton Landing Park. Critic Clement Greenberg, lawyer Ira Lowe, and artist Robert Motherwell named in Smith's will as executors of his estate.

Plates

Plate 1 *Ad Mare,* 1939 (cat. 35)

Plate 2 *Untitled* (Virgin Islands shell
and map landscape), 1933 (cat. 5)

Plate 3 *Untitled* (neo-constructivist landscape), 1930 (cat. 1)

Plate 4 *Aerial Construction*, 1936 (cat. 27)

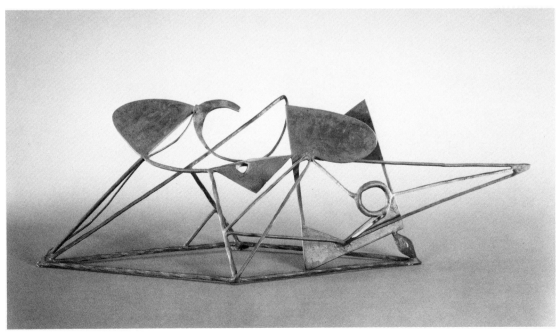

Plate 5 *Untitled* (Virgin Islands relief), 1932 (cat. 4)

Plate 6 *Untitled* (patchwork landscape), c. 1930 (cat. 2)

Plate 7 *Untitled* (desert skeletons), 1936 (cat. 9)

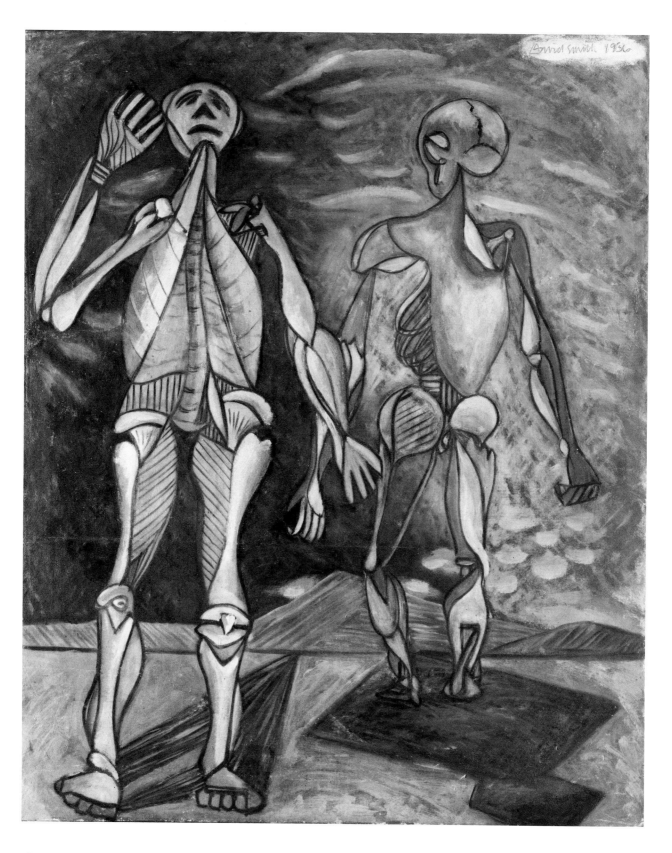

Plate 12 *Construction*, 1932 (cat. 24)   Plate 13 *Head*, 1932 (cat. 25)

Plate 14 *Untitled* (cubist nude), c. 1930 (cat. 17)

Plate 15 *Untitled* (green linear nude), c. 1964 (cat. 132)

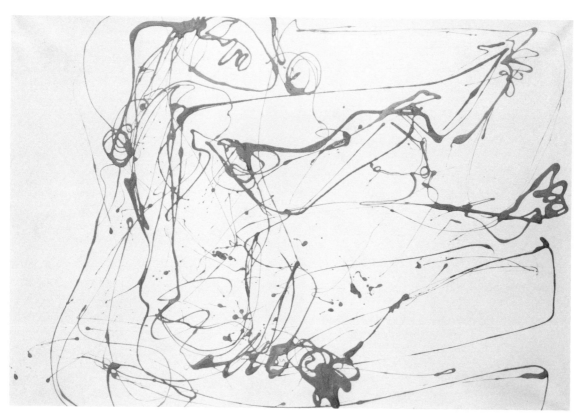

Plate 16 *Reclining Figure,*
1939–40 (cat. 40)

Plate 17 *Untitled* (seated nude,
lower torso), c. 1964 (cat. 135)

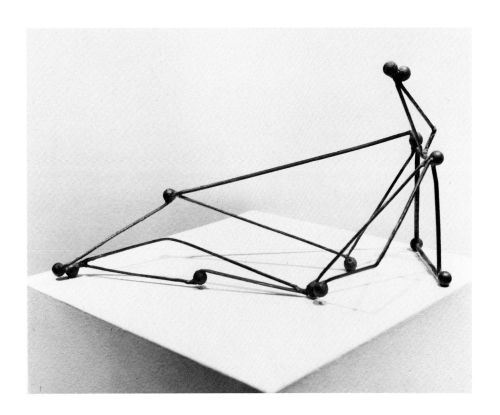

Plate 18 *Untitled* (nude), 1964 (cat. 151)

Plate 19 *Untitled* (lavender nude), c. 1964 (cat. 133)

Plate 20 *Untitled* (flying bony figures), c. 1934 (cat. 21)

Plate 21 *Head as a Still Life I,* 1942 (cat. 63)

Plate 22 *Bent Blade Plane,* 1936 (cat. 28)

Plate 23 *Untitled* (gestural sculpture); 1937 (cat. 15)

Plate 24 *Untitled* (reclining figure), 1939–40 (cat. 22)

Plate 25 *Blue Construction,* 1938 (cat. 32)

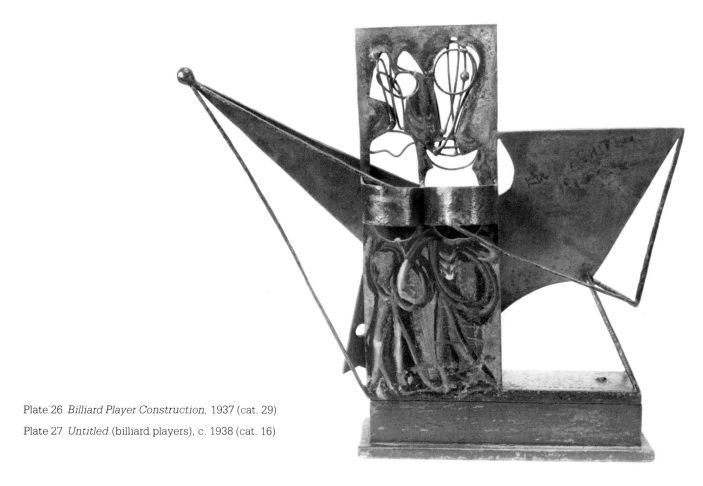

Plate 26 *Billiard Player Construction,* 1937 (cat. 29)
Plate 27 *Untitled* (billiard players), c. 1938 (cat. 16)

Plate 28 *Untitled* (billiard players), c. 1936 (cat. 12)

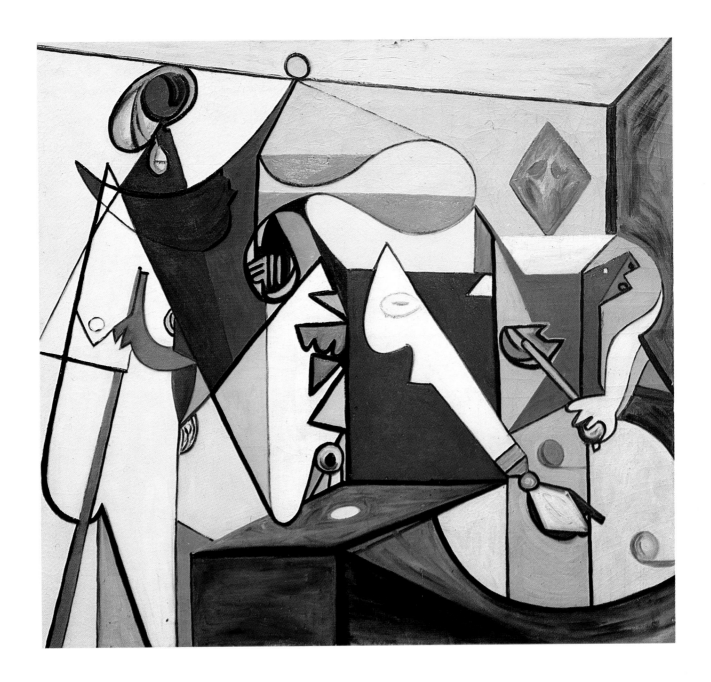

Plate 29 *Untitled* (billiard player), 1946 (cat. 42)

Plate 30 *Billiard Player III*, 1945 (cat. 65)

Plate 31 *Untitled,* 1937 (cat. 31)

Plate 32 *Untitled* (two heads), 1936 (cat. 10)

Plate 33 *Suspended Cube,* 1938 (cat. 34)

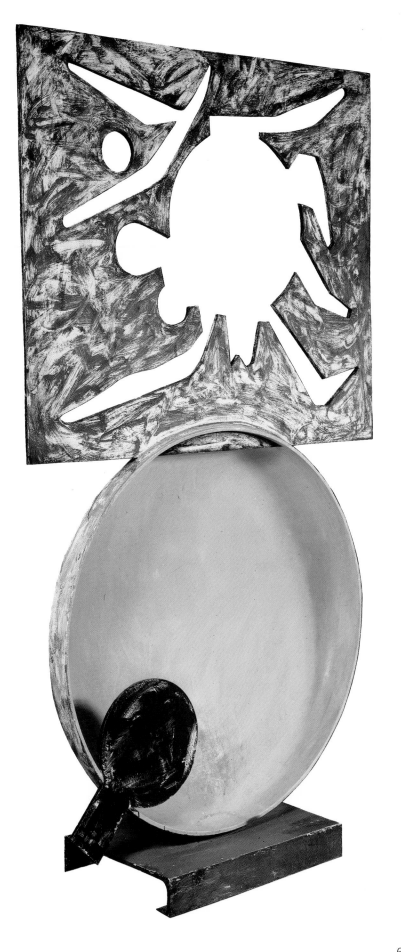

Plate 34 *7 Hours*, 1961 (cat. 155)

Plate 35 *Untitled* (surrealist creatures), 1946 (cat. 53)

Plate 36 *Untitled* (two bony figures), 1946 (cat. 45)

Plate 37 *Eagle's Lair,* 1948 (cat. 72)

Plate 38 *Untitled* (landscape with *Eagle's Lair),* 1946 (cat. 44)

Plate 39 *Untitled (Terpsichore and Euterpe
in landscape)*, 1947 (cat. 48)

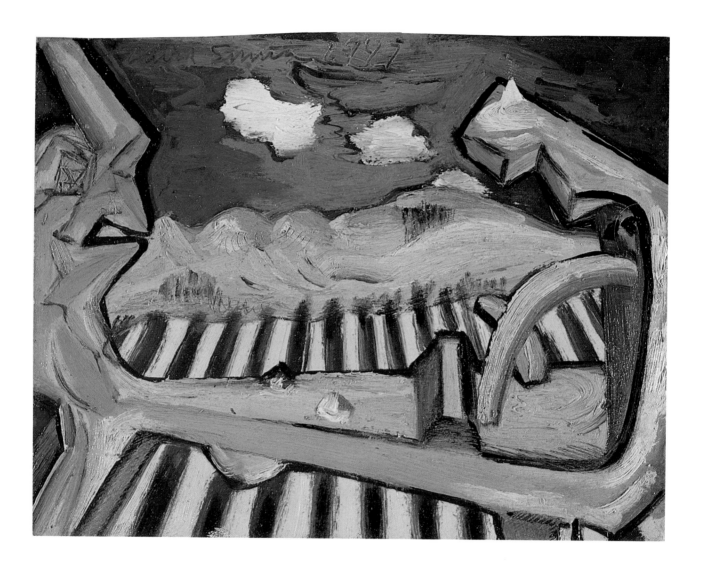

Plate 40 *Cello Player,* c. 1946 (cat. 46)

Plate 41 *Untitled (Terpsichore and Euterpe),* 1946 (cat. 54)

Plate 42 *Drawing for Beach Scene,* 1946 (cat. 55)

Plate 43 *Cello Player*, 1946 (cat. 69)

Plate 44 *Piat*, 1946 (cat. 41)

Plate 45 *Untitled,* 1954 (cat. 113)

Plate 46 *Helmholtzian Landscape,* 1946 (cat. 70)

Plate 47 *Untitled* (multisculptural study), 1944 (cat. 51)

Plate 48 *Drawing for Sculpture,* 1934 (cat. 20)

Plate 49 *Leda,* 1938 (cat. 33)

Plate 50 *Untitled* (bony dancers), 1937 (cat. 14)

Plate 51 *Untitled (Home of the Welder),* c. 1946 (cat. 56)

Plate 52 *Home of the Welder,* 1945 (cat. 67)

Plate 53 *Untitled* (mountain landscape), c. 1957 (cat. 81)

Plate 54 *Untitled* (black abstraction), 1960 (cat. 137)

Plate 55 *Untitled* (mountain landscape), 1957 (cat. 100)

Plate 56 *Untitled* (reclining nude), 1963 (cat. 150)

Plate 57 *Steel Drawing I,* 1945 (cat. 68)

85

Plate 58 *Untitled* (color abstraction), 1960 (cat. 138)

Plate 59 *Black White Forward,* 1961 (cat. 153)

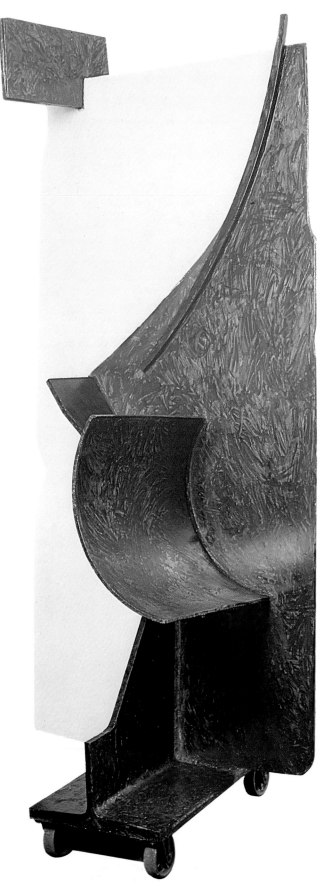

Plate 60 *Ballet*, 1941 (cat. 58)

Plate 61 *At the Bar*, 1941 (cat. 61)

Plate 62 *Untitled* (dancers), 1946 (cat. 43)

Plate 63 *White Egg with Pink,*
1958 (cat. 82)

Plate 64 *Untitled* (organic abstraction), 1952 (cat. 90)

Plate 65 *Untitled* (shower of strokes), 1958 (cat. 102)

Plate 66 *Wild Plum,* 1956 (cat. 120)

Plate 67 *Untitled* (day-glo eclipse), c. 1962 (cat. 143)

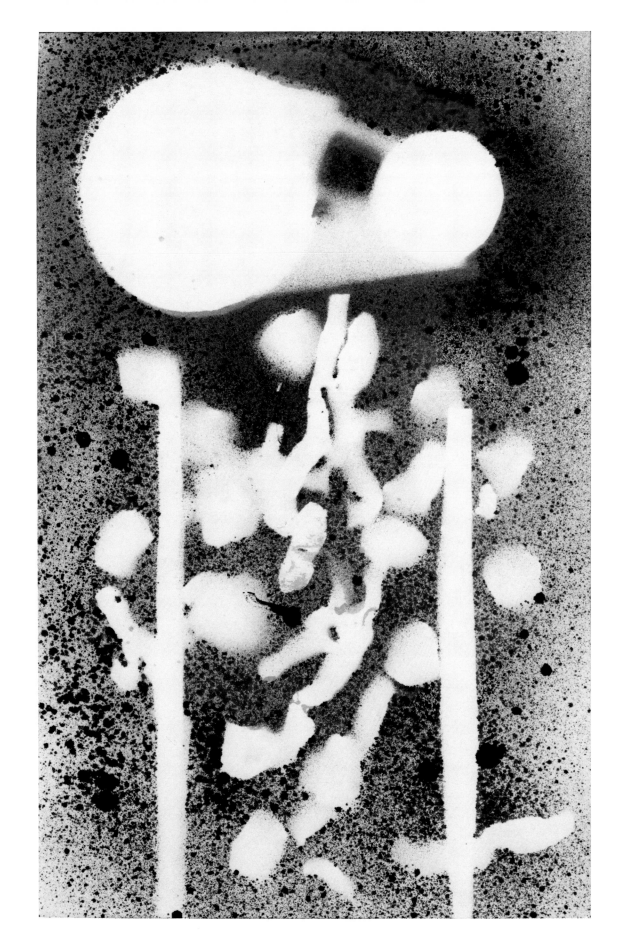

Plate 68 *Untitled* (relief with bones), 1956 (cat. 77)

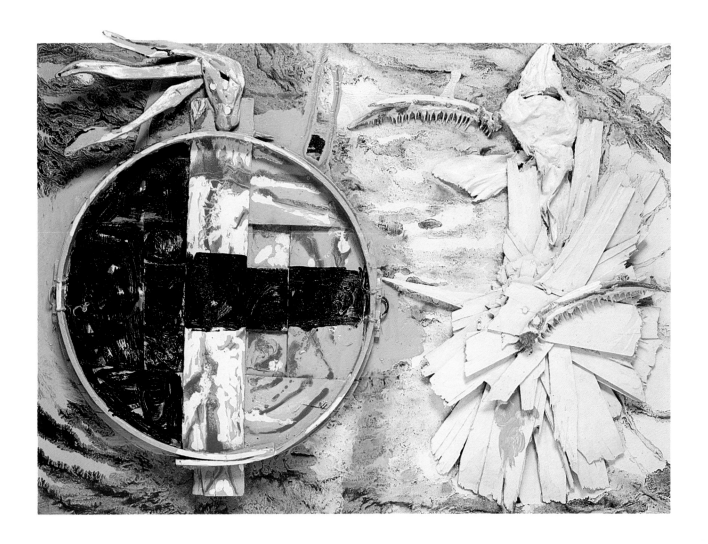

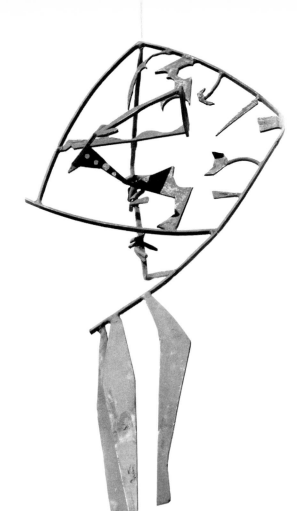

Plate 70 *Parallel 42,* 1953 (cat. 110)

Plate 71 *Untitled* (transparent skull-like sculpture), 1952 (cat. 92)

Plate 72 *Untitled* (floating galaxy), c. 1959 (cat. 88)

Plate 73 *Star Cage,* 1950 (cat. 107)

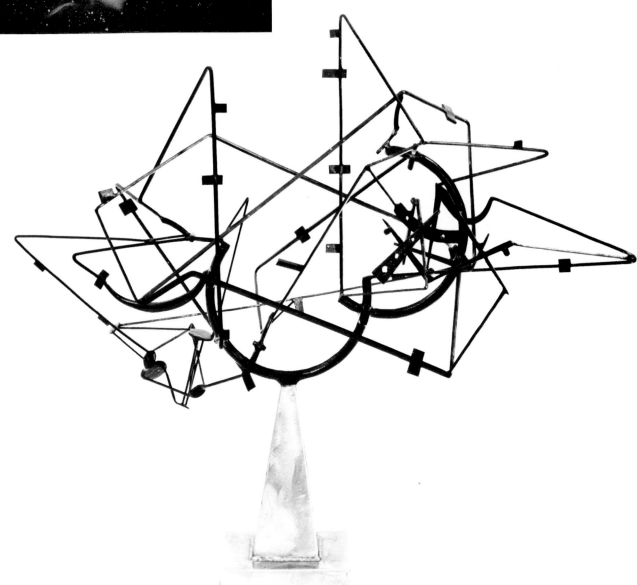

Plate 74 *Untitled* (rectangles on sable ground), c. 1962 (cat. 148)

Plate 75 *Timeless Clock,* 1957 (cat. 122)

Plate 76 *Cockfight Variation 2,* c. 1945 (cat. 52)

Plate 77 *Cockfight,* 1945 (cat. 66)

Plate 78 *Agricola IX,* 1952 (cat. 109)

Plate 79 *Chicken Bones,* 1951 (cat. 89)

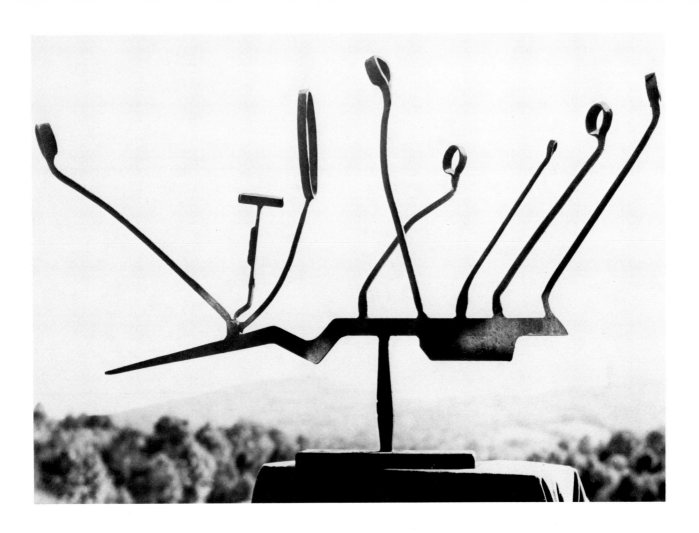

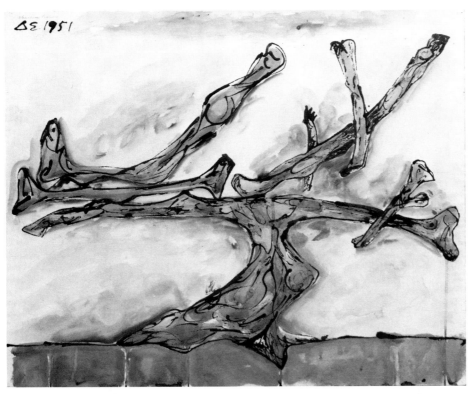

Plate 80 *Untitled* (elevated sculptural form), 1953 (cat. 93)

Plate 81 *Untitled* (calligraphy), 1958 (cat. 101)

Plate 82 *Royal Bird,* 1948 (cat. 73)

Plate 83 *Australia*, 1951 (cat. 108)

Plate 84 *Untitled* (curvilinear sculptures), c. 1953 (cat. 96)

Plate 85 *Untitled* (rectangular and cubic sculptures), c. 1955 (cat. 97)

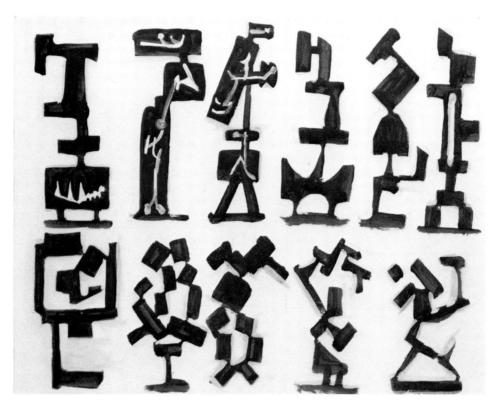

Plate 86 *Untitled* (four totemic sculptures), 1956 (cat. 75)

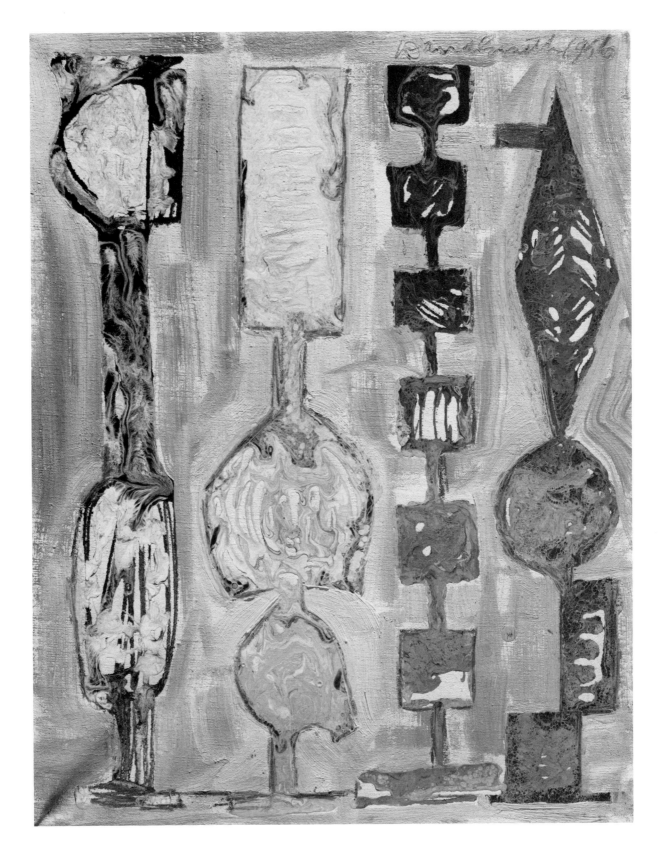

Plate 87 *Lonesome Man,* 1957 (cat. 121)

Plate 89 *Untitled* (vertical sculpture), 1961 (cat. 140)

Plate 88 *Untitled* (collage for *Fifteen Planes*), 1957 (cat. 78)

Plate 90 *Untitled* (study for *Superstructure on 4*), 1959 (cat. 103)

Plate 91 *Auburn Queen,* 1959 (cat. 124)

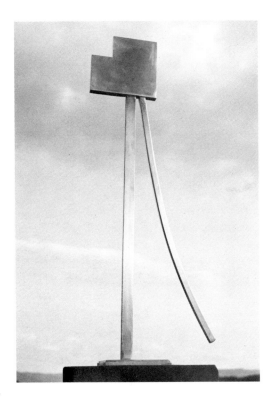

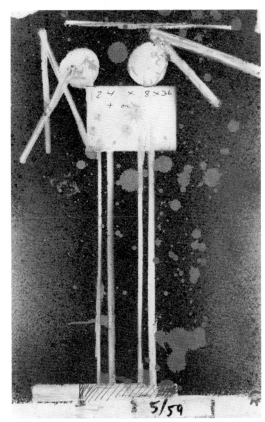

Plate 92 *Untitled* (horizontal sculpture), c. 1960 (cat. 139)

Plate 93 *Untitled* (free-floating image), c. 1963 (cat. 128)

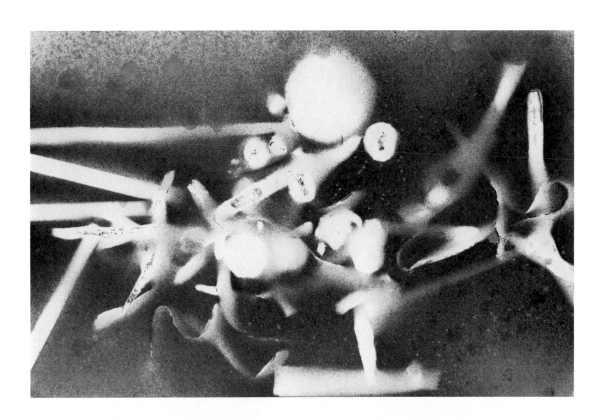

Plate 94 *Bolton Landing*, 1961 (cat. 154)

Plate 95 *Raven II,* 1955 (cat. 117)

Plate 96 *Untitled* (related to *Raven),* 1953 (cat. 95)

Plate 97 *Tanktotem IV*, 1953 (cat. 111)

Plate 98 *Untitled* (futurist figure), c. 1961 (cat. 141)

Plate 99 *Night Window*, 1959 (cat. 87)

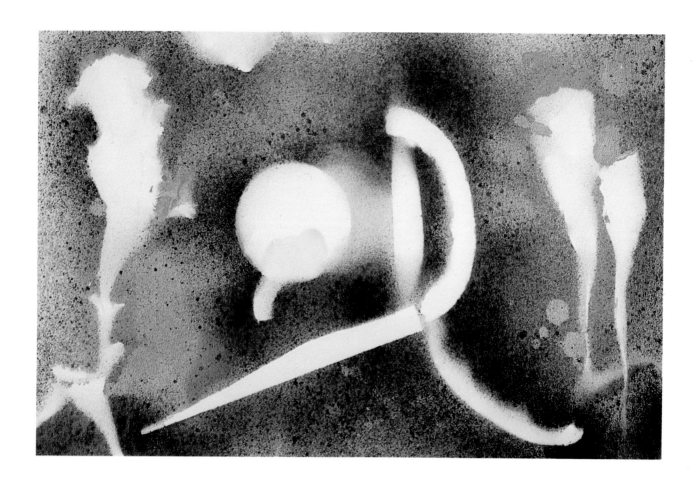

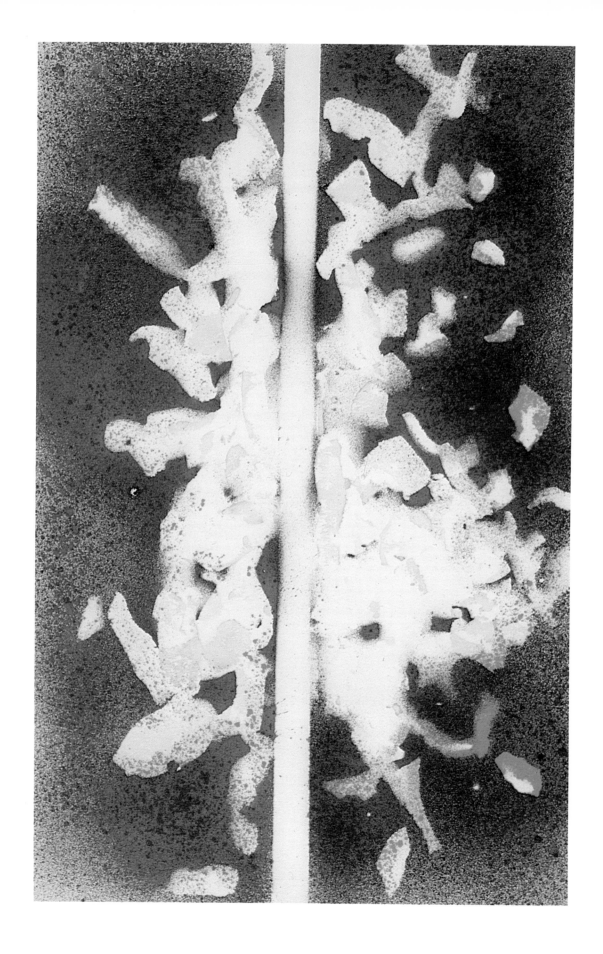

Plate 102 *Voltri I,* 1962 (cat. 157)

Plate 103 *Untitled* (standing woman, profile), 1956 (cat. 76)

Plate 104 *Untitled* (skeletal network), c. 1958 (cat. 83)

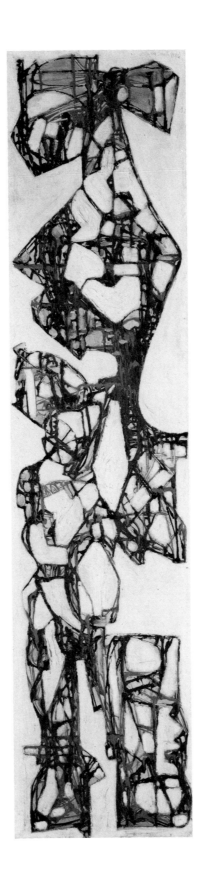

Plate 105 *Yellow Vertical,* 1955 (cat. 118)

Plate 106 *Study in Arcs,* 1959 (cat. 125)

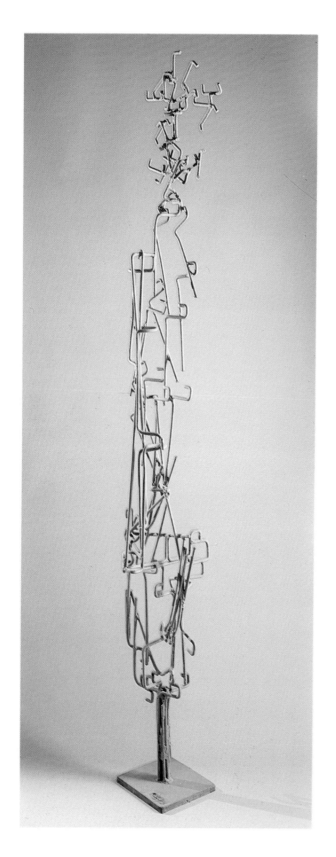

Plate 107 *Menand VI,* 1963 (cat. 159)

Plate 108 *Bronze Planes 3/9/64,* 1964 (cat. 162)

Plate 109 *Untitled (2 Circle IV),* c. 1962 (cat. 149)

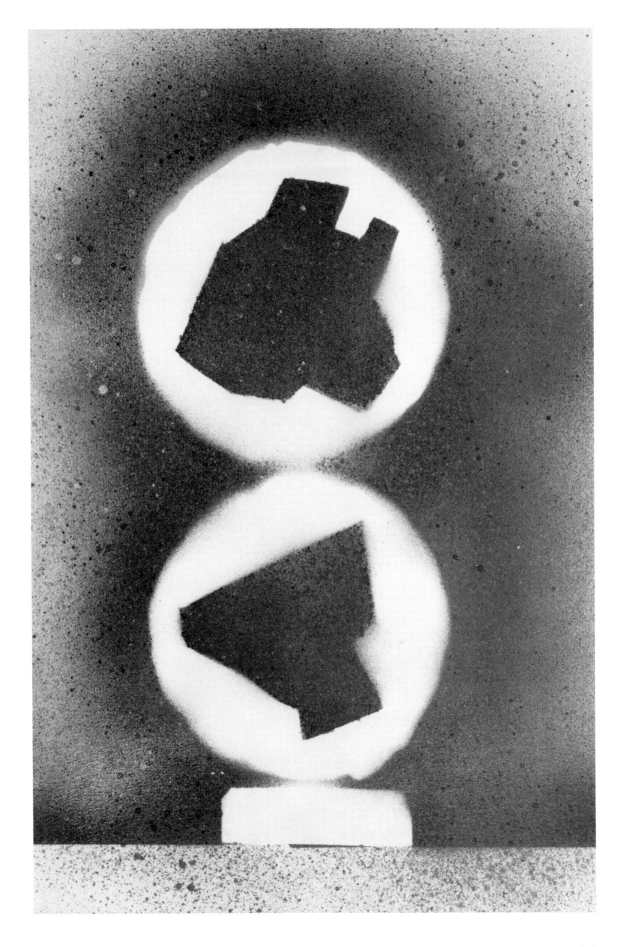

Plate 110 *Untitled* (overlapping planes), c. 1963 (cat. 129)   Plate 111 *Zig IV,* 1961 (cat. 156)

   Plate 110 *Untitled* (overlapping planes), c. 1963 (cat. 129)   Plate 111 *Zig IV,* 1961 (cat. 156)

Plate 112 *Untitled (Cubi XIX),* 1964 (cat. 131)

Plate 113 *Untitled* (rectangular bars), c. 1964 (cat. 134)

Plate 114 *Untitled (Zig VII),* 1962 (cat. 126)

Plate 115 *Becca,* 1965 (cat. 163)

Plate 116 *Volton XIV,* 1963 (cat. 160)

Plate 117 *Cubi XII,* 1963 (cat. 161)

Annotated Catalog of the Exhibition

The catalog is organized chronologically by decade, and within each decade works are listed according to medium. Dimensions are given in centimeters (and inches), height x width x depth.

All works not otherwise credited are in the collection of Candida and Rebecca Smith, New York.

Paintings 1930s

1 _Untitled_ (neo-constructivist landscape) Plate 3
1930; oil on canvas; 61 x 40.6 (24 x 16); Estate 75.30.28

2 _Untitled_ (patchwork landscape) Plate 6
c. 1930; oil on canvas; 30.5 x 40.6 (12 x 16); Estate 75.30.45

For Smith, landscape was seen from an aerial perspective. He wrote: "Today the landscape may be viewed on a cross country journey from a plane three miles up. Looking down there is no space. The solid earth, its rocks and hills become an endless flat plane. Houses, factories, hard objects, solids become only pattern. Rivers, highways, man-made boundaries are flowing graceful sweeping lines opposed by spots of lakes and squares of fields. The view from space makes solid form appear pattern."[1]

3 _Untitled_ (Virgin Islands landscape with boat)
1932; oil on wood; 40 x 32.4 (15¾ x 12¾)
Dorothy Dehner, New York

4 _Untitled_ (Virgin Islands relief) Plate 5
1932; oil on wood with wooden pieces; 45.7 x 57.2 (18 x 22½); Estate 75.30.136

Although Smith moved directly from painting to sculpture, his early reliefs are important in that they transfer the thematic and stylistic concerns of the early paintings into sculpture. This is one of several painted reliefs that Smith produced at the beginning of his career. He later wrote: "My student period was only involved with painting. The painting developed into raised levels from the canvas. Gradually the canvas became the base, and the painting was a sculpture. I have never recognized any separation except one element of dimension....I do not recognize the limits where painting ends and sculpture begins."[2]

1. Gray, _David Smith by David Smith_, p. 71.

2. McCoy, _David Smith_, p. 82.

5 _Untitled_ (Virgin Islands shell and map landscape) Plate 2
1933; oil on canvas; 66 x 91.4 (26 x 36); Estate 75.30.90

Comparison of this painting with a relief (cat. 4), drawings (cat. 18, 19), sculptures (cat. 24, 25), and another painting (cat. 3) shows how Smith typically pursued a theme through a variety of permutations. Factors that remain constant are the prominence of planar silhouettes, the ambiguous overlapping of transparent and opaque planes, and the use of the wandering line whose movement is independent of any descriptive function.

6 _Untitled_ (bather)
1934; oil on canvas; 88.9 x 101.6 (35 x 40); Estate 75.30.85

7 _Untitled_ (bathers)
1934; oil on canvas; 43.8 x 43.6 (17¼ x 16¹⁵⁄₁₆); Estate 75.30.69

8 _Untitled_ (twirling forms)
1935; oil on canvas; 88.6 x 71.1 (34⅞ x 28); Estate 75.30.106

9 _Untitled_ (desert skeletons) Plate 7
1936; oil on canvas; 90.2 x 76.2 (35½ x 30); Estate 75.30.151

10 _Untitled_ (two heads) Plate 32
1936; oil, egg tempera on wood; 38.1 x 46 (15 x 18⅛); Estate 73.30.124
Hirshhorn Museum and Sculpture Garden, Washington, D.C., purchase, 1976

11 _Untitled_ (planar sculpture)
1936; oil on Masonite; 35.6 x 44.5 (14 x 17½); Estate 75.30.118

12 _Untitled_ (billiard players) Plate 28
c. 1936; oil on canvas; 119.4 x 132 (47 x 52); Estate 75.30.146

13 _Untitled_ (still life)
c. 1936; oil on canvas; 66 x 71.1 (26 x 28); Estate 75.30.75

14 _Untitled_ (bony dancers) Plate 50
1937; oil on canvas; 92.1 x 81.3 (36¼ x 32); Estate 75.30.76

Smith's fascination with bony skeletal forms is evident throughout his career. The metamorphic merging of two bodies and the sightly macabre humor that pervades this depiction are characteristic of Smith's brand of surrealism in the thirties and forties. The implication of twisting

movement is extended into a full-fledged *figura serpentina* in *Leda* (cat. 33) of the following year.

15 *Untitled* (gestural sculpture) Plate 23
1937; oil on canvas; 68.3 x 88 (26⅞ x 34¹⁵⁄₁₆); Estate 75.30.77

One of Smith's ambitions was to convey in sculpture the free movement of forms in space, as it could be achieved in painting. The sculpture envisioned here is more free and gestural than *Bent Blade Plane* of 1936 (cat. 28). The use of color reinforces this liveliness. Indeed, Smith spoke of "movement and the color of movement by Matisse."[3] In this painting, color distinguishes the separate elements of the sculpture and sets up a dynamic relationship among them, as it does in his later sculptures.

16 *Untitled* (billiard players) Plate 27
c. 1938; oil on paperboard; 29.2 x 22.9 (11½ x 9); Estate 75.30.132

Between 1935 and 1946, Smith depicted billiard players in seven paintings (cat. 12, 16), four major sculptures (cat. 29, 32, 65), and countless drawings that are variously realistic, cubist, and surrealist in style. A lively interchange among the various media evolved as Smith shifted his emphasis from the highly stylized abstraction evident in this painting, to volumetric structure, to planar collage. Inspired perhaps by his own enjoyment of the game, he collected magazine and newspaper photographs of the great billiard players of his day; key elements of these pictures were incorporated into his works.

Drawings 1930s

17 *Untitled* (cubist nude) Plate 14
c. 1930; gouache, watercolor, pencil on paper; 29.5 x 22 (11⅝ x 8⅝); Estate 73.30.3

This studio nude reflects the training Smith received from Kimon Nicolaides and Jan Matulka at the Art Students League, as well as the schematic, somewhat literal synthetic cubism that was prevalent in the United States at the time. The equalization of form and space, and the emphasis on planar contour remained constant in Smith's work.

18 *Untitled* (Virgin Islands coral and shell)
1931; brush, pen and ink, pencil on paper; 44.1 x 73.2 (17⅜ x 28⅞); Estate 73.31.2

3. David Smith Papers, roll N.D.4, frame 0842.

19 *Untitled* (Virgin Islands map) Plate 11
1933; gouache on paper; 45.3 x 60.8 (17⅞ x 24); Estate 73.33.4

David Smith's 1931–32 sojourn in the Virgin Islands with Dorothy Dehner marked his transition from art student to artist. This drawing is one of many works with Caribbean imagery he produced during his stay and after his return to New York. The transparent planes and free-flowing lines suggest but do not strictly define form. The overall maplike patterning relates to the schematic coastal views of other drawings and paintings (cat. 3) and offers a curious premonition of Smith's great landscape sculpture of the fifties, *Hudson River Landscape* (fig. 8).

20 *Drawing for Sculpture* Plate 48
1934; pen and ink, gouache on paper; 28.2 x 21.6 (11 x 8½); Estate 73.34.14

21 *Untitled* (flying bony figures) Plate 20
c. 1934; pen and ink, oil on paper; 26.6 x 36.6 (10½ x 14⅜); Estate 73.36.3

Smith felt that the absence of gravity in drawings and paintings was "a great liberation and has provided the conceptual break from chiaroscuro and the sculptural concept in general."[4]

22 *Untitled* (reclining figure) Plate 24
1939-40; gouache, black conté crayon, watercolor, pencil on blue paper; 30.5 x 45.6 (12 x 18); Estate 73.40.4

Photograph 1930s

23 *Untitled* (abstraction)
c. 1932; photograph from collaged negative; 20.3 x 25.4 (8 x 10)
David Smith Papers (Box 24), loaned to the Archives of American Art, Washington, D.C., by Candida and Rebecca Smith.

Sculpture 1930s

24 *Construction* Plate 12
1932; wood, wire, nails, coral, painted red, blue, yellow; 94.3 x 41.3 x 18.4 (37⅛ x 16¼ x 7¼); base: 4.4 x 24.1 x 30.5 (1¾ x 9½ x 12)

The mixture of materials in this sculpture represents the

4. Ibid., roll N.D.4, frame 0991.

transference from painting to sculpture of the textural differentiation of form that Smith learned from Jan Matulka, who encouraged heavily textured picture surfaces. This piece combines many of the interests that Smith later developed into distinct kinds of sculpture: drawing in space, geometric volumes, and sculpture defined by color and texture.

25 *Head*   Plate 13
1932; wood, painted black, red, white, green; 58.4 x 21.3 x 13.7 (23 x 8⅜ x 5⅜); base: 8.9 x 16.5 x 16.5 (3½ x 6½ x 6½)

Smith transformed his Virgin Island drawings and paintings into sculpture by using a freestanding piece of wood as the support, applying several planes at right angles to the synthetic cubist surface, and making the wandering line determine its contour.

26 *Agricola Head*
1933; iron and steel, painted red; 46.7 x 25.7 x 19.7 (18⅜ x 10⅛ x 7¾); base: 7.9 x 25.4 x 18.4 (3⅛ x 10 x 7¼)

27 *Aerial Construction*   Plate 4
1936; iron, painted terra-cotta; 25.1 x 78.4 x 29 (10 x 30⅞ x 11½)
Hirshhorn Museum and Sculpture Garden, Washington, D.C.

Much of Smith's sculpture depends more on line and plane, means of painting and drawing, than on mass or implied volume. Like this early work, many sculptures are derived from his 1930s cubist paintings in their reduction of form and space to line and plane, in their rhythmic alternation of solid and negative planes, in the non-naturalistic dislocation of forms, and in a shifting illusion of depth.

28 *Bent Blade Plane*   Plate 22
1936; iron; 45.4 x 55.6 x 34.3 (17⅞ x 21⅞ x 13½)

One of David Smith's greatest achievements was to incorporate into sculpture gestural lines and planes that were as expressive as those traditionally found in two dimensions.

29 *Billiard Player Construction*   Plate 26
1937; iron and encaustic; 43.8 x 52.1 x 16.2 (17¼ x 20½ x 6⅜); base: 5.1 x 40.6 x 15.2 (2 x 16 x 6)
Dr. and Mrs. Arthur E. Kahn, New York

30 *Interior*
1937; steel and bronze, painted red oxide; 38.7 x 66.0 x 13.3 (15¼ x 26 x 5¼); base: 9.2 x 41.9 x 13.3 (3⅜ x 26½ x 5¼)
Weatherspoon Art Gallery, University of North Carolina at Greensboro, anonymous gift, 1979

31 *Untitled*   Plate 31
1937; iron, painted orange, red, pink, white, black, brown, blue; 29.8 x 41.9 x 14.6 (11¾ x 16½ x 5¾)
Frank Stella, New York

32 *Blue Construction*   Plate 25
1938; steel, painted blue, black; 92.1 x 72.4 x 76.2 (36¼ x 28½ x 30); base: 11.8 x 46.1 x 39.4 (4⅝ x 18⅜ x 15½)

Smith believed that "color has a psychological appeal, especially in its relation to form. As there exists a logic in the scale of sculpture, there exists a color. There must be perfect unity between the idea, the substance, the color and the dimension."[5] In this work, the baked enamel surface of loosely brushed gestural strokes, black over blue, enlivens the active, angular volumes that define the sculpture. Although the piece appears to be abstract, its similarity to a sculpture depicted in a painting of the same period (cat. 16) suggests its association with Smith's billiard player series.

33 *Leda*   Plate 49
1938; steel, painted brown; 73.7 x 32.1 x 45.1 (29 x 12⅝ x 17¾)
Museum of Fine Arts, Houston, gift of Mr. and Mrs. W. D. Hawkins

34 *Suspended Cube*   Plate 33
1938; steel, aluminum paint; 58.4 x 40.6 x 51.4 (23 x 16 x 20¼); base: 34.9 (13¾) diameter
Dr. Henry Grunebaum, Cambridge, Massachusetts

In this piece Smith articulates many of the concerns he explored on a far grander scale in the *Cubi* series more than two decades later. This witty sculpture combines a daring suspension of forms in space with a play of solid and negative volumes, asymmetrical balance, inherent monumentality, and light-reflective surfaces.

35 *Ad Mare*   Plate 1 [Not in exhibition]
1939; steel; 76.2 x 71.1 x 22.9 (20 x 28 x 9)
Sibley Smith, Wakefield, Rhode Island

36 *Growing Forms*
1939; cast aluminum on rod; 100.4 x 21.6 x 16.5 (39½ x 8½ x 6½)

5. Ibid., roll N.D.5, frame 0019.

37 *Medal for Dishonor: Munitions Makers* Plate 8
1939; bronze; 25 (10) diameter

Of the numerous works that Smith executed between 1936 and 1947 to protest the circumstances of war, his fifteen *Medals for Dishonor* are the most powerful statement of his concerns. These medallions, like his other works on this theme, combine caricature with surrealist irrationality in order to shock and compel the viewer's response to their message. In contrast to Smith's 1932 painted reliefs (cat. 4), which were derived from cubist collage and assemblage, the sculptural reliefs he executed in the late thirties, the forties, and the mid-fifties developed from the numismatic tradition.

38 *Medal for Dishonor: Death by Gas*
1939–40; bronze; 29.2 x 26.7 (11½ x 10½)
Hirshhorn Museum and Sculpture Garden, Washington, D.C.

39 *Medal for Dishonor: Propaganda for War*
1939–40; bronze; 28.7 x 24.5 (11⅜ x 9⅝)
Hirshhorn Museum and Sculpture Garden, Washington, D.C.

40 *Reclining Figure* Plate 16
1939–40; iron rods, steel; 24.1 x 43.2 x 20.3 (9½ x 17 x 8)
André Emmerich Gallery, New York

Line is used in Smith's sculpture, as in his drawings, as form reduced to its essence, as contour, and as gesture for its own sake. Comparison of this early "drawing in space" to a drawing on paper of a similar, though volumetric sculptural figure (cat. 22) reveals the agility and spatial complexity of this work.

Paintings 1940s

41 *Piat* Plate 44
1946; oil on Masonite; 59.7 x 75.2 (23½ x 29⅝); Estate 75.46.3

Among Smith's papers on loan to the Archives of American Art are newspaper photographs of the cello players Emanuel Feuermann and Gregor Piatigorsky, whose celli and long-fingered hands appear prominently in Smith's paintings and sculpture. This surrealist fantasy reveals the first steps in the amalgamation of figure and instrument seen in a subsequent painting (cat. 46) as an elegant, romantically colored sculpture. This hybrid form is further stylized in the final sculpture (cat. 69), which nonetheless retains the grace and humanity of its painted counterparts.

42 *Untitled* (billiard player) Plate 29
1946; oil on paper, mounted on Masonite; 77.5 x 56.8 (30½ x 22⅜); Estate 75.46.9

This humorous depiction of a billiard player as some sort of mad scientist, surrounded by the apparatus of his trade, is considerably more animated than the sculptural version of the same image (cat. 29) that preceded it. The two are alike in the synthesis of figure and environment into a single structural image, the effective use of outline and contour, and the staccato rhyming of form.

43 *Untitled* (dancers) Plate 62
1946; oil on Masonite; 51.4 x 66.7 (20¼ x 26¼); Estate 75.46.15

44 *Untitled* (landscape with *Eagle's Lair)* Plate 38
1946; oil on paperboard; 60.3 x 75.6 (23¾ x 29¾); Estate 75.46.4

This work provides a good example of one of the ways in which Smith generated images in paintings and drawings that subsequently were transformed into sculpture. The mood of mystery and abandon that prevails in this lifeless landscape is sustained in the bronze *Eagles Lair,* 1948 (cat. 72), which replicates the cagelike relic on the right of this picture.

45 *Untitled* (two bony figures) Plate 36
1946; oil on paperboard; 59.1 x 76.2 (23¼ x 30); Estate 75.46.10

46 *Cello Player* Plate 40
c. 1946; oil on Masonite; 57.5 x 77.2 (25⅝ x 30⅜); Estate 75.46.1

47 *Untitled* (four musicians)
1946–47; oil on Masonite; 77.2 x 56.8 (30⅜ x 22⅜); Estate 75.46.2

48 *Untitled (Terpsichore and Euterpe* in landscape)
Plate 39
1947; oil on paperboard; 18.3 x 23.5 (7³⁄₁₆ x 9¼); Estate 75.30.128

Smith treated the subject of Terpsichore and Euterpe in paintings, drawings (cat. 54), and sculpture, variously showing the metamorphosis of dancer, piano, and piano player into a single sculptural form. In this portrayal of the 1947 sculpture *Terpsichore and Euterpe,* he shows the work as he may have positioned it on the windowsill of his living room or on the wall that ran along the porch behind his home, with the Adirondack mountains just behind. The impression conveyed by this composition, and by

Smith's photograph of the sculpture (cat. 60), is of monumentality considerably greater than the sculpture's actual size.

Drawings 1940s

49 *Untitled* *(Medal for Dishonor: Munitions Makers)* Plate 9
1940; pen and ink, colored ink, colored crayon on paper; 33.9 x 49.5 (13⅜ x 19½); Estate 73.38.15

Smith's drawings frequently contain a mixture of improvisation and exact rendering when compared to related sculptures. A skeleton taken from a 1936 painting (cat. 9) and motifs incorporated in *Death by Gas* (cat. 38) are included in this drawing, as well as the essential elements of the *Munitions Makers* medallion (cat. 37) on which this drawing is based.

50 *Aryan Fold* Plate 10
1943; pen and ink on paper; 50.0 x 64.2 (19¾ x 25¼); Estate 73.43.1

51 *Untitled* (multisculptural study) Plate 47
1944; pen and ink, watercolor, pencil on paper; 49.8 x 64.3 (19⅝ x 25⅜); Estate 73.44.1

This drawing shows the genesis of the bony, biomorphic sculptures that Smith executed in the mid-forties. Most curious is the addition of wheeled bases to the sculpturesque forms, which represents a midpoint between Smith's implication of movement in dancers, bathers, and running figures and the use of real wheels on sculpture, beginning with *Sentinel III* in 1957 (fig. 7).

52 *Cockfight Variation 2* Plate 76
c. 1945; pen and ink, wash, pastel on paper; 63.5 x 50 (25 x 19¾); Estate 73.44.4

53 *Untitled* (surrealist creatures) Plate 35
1946; tempera on paper; 55.9 x 82.5 (22 x 30¼); Estate 73.46.2
Whitney Museum of American Art, New York, gift of the Lauder Foundation—Drawing Fund, 1979

54 *Untitled* (Terpsichore and Euterpe) Plate 41
1946; oil, pen and ink on paper; 58.3 x 74.1 (23 x 29¼); Estate 73.46.6

55 *Drawing for Beach Scene* Plate 42
1946; oil, gouache, pen and ink on paper; 51.4 x 66.4 (21¼ x 26⅛); Estate 73.46.4

56 *Untitled* *(Home of the Welder)* Plate 51
c. 1946; gouache on paper; 58.0 x 73.9 (22⅞ x 29⅛); Estate 73.46.5

Like the earlier sculpture of the same theme (cat. 67), this drawing shows a psychic inventory of David Smith's home life. The structures depicted in both drawing and sculpture are alike in their compartmentalization, skeletal roof, and nautical motifs. The emotional differences between the two images are reinforced by the rigidity of the sculptural material and the colorful fluidity of gouache.

Etchings 1940s

57 *Ballet*
1941; etching; 9.9 x 14.8 (3⅞ x 5⅞); Estate 77.41.1G

58 *Ballet* Plate 60
1941; steel etching plate; 10.1 x 15.2 (4 x 6); Estate 77.41.1

Throughout the thirties and forties, dancers were one of Smith's favorite subjects. In the *Ballet* etching, in the sculpture *At the Bar*, 1941 (cat. 61), and in an untitled painting from 1946 (cat. 43), the dancers are similar in structure and pose. They differ in the suggestion of movement, which is most convincing in the lyrical painting. The sculptural quality of the etching can be seen by comparing the plate from which it was printed with the planar steel sculpture *Steel Drawing I*, 1945 (cat. 68), which it may have inspired. Smith's prints were always closer to sculpture than drawing because of his treatment of the plates.

59 *Woman in War*
1941; etching; 17.2 x 22.3 (6¾ x 8¾); Estate 77.41.2b

Photograph 1940s

60 *Untitled* (Terpsichore and Euterpe)
1947; photograph; 20.3 x 25.4 (8 x 10)
David Smith Papers (Box 34), loaned to the Archives of American Art, Washington, D.C., by Candida and Rebecca Smith

David Smith's photographic interpretation of his sculpture constitutes a significant body of work in its own right. His photographs—many of which illustrate this catalog—give a unique opportunity to view Smith's sculpture as he wanted them seen. By photographing a sculpture outdoors, seen from below and surrounded by vast space, Smith made his sculptures appear larger, more immaterial, and more complex, irrespective of their actual size and character.

Sculpture 1940s

61 *At the Bar* Plate 61
1941; bronze on wooden base; 19.1 x 19.7 x 10.8 (7½ x 7¾ x 4¼); base: 4.4 x 24.1 x 21.6 (1¾ x 9½ x 8½)
Ann and Robert Freedman, New York

62 *Bathers*
1942; bronze; 24.1 x 22.9 x 11.4 (9½ x 9 x 4½)

63 *Head as a Still Life I* Plate 21
1942; cast aluminum on wooden base; 21.6 x 30.5 x 11.4 (8½ x 12 x 4½); base: 5.1 x 23.5 x 15.9 (2 x 9¼ x 6¼)
Des Moines Art Center, gift of Jesse R. Fillman, Boston, in honor of James S. Schramm, 1977

Bony, biomorphic forms were common in Smith's paintings, drawings, and sculpture of the forties, continuing the surrealist vein that had existed in his work since 1934. This cast aluminum sculpture relates formally to a lumbering bather depicted in an early painting (cat. 6), yet the title suggests a more complex meaning. Such titles as *Head as a Still Life* and *Figure as Landscape* indicate Smith's desire to break down established genres of art. This ambition parallels his aim to overcome the limitations inherent in painting, sculpture, and drawing by making "drawings in space," sculptural etchings, and what Smith termed "sculpture painted." [6]

64 *Aftermath Figure*
1945; bronze on steel base; 34 x 19.4 x 7.6 (13⅜ x 7⅝ x 3); base: 1.6 x 7.6 x 11.8 (⅝ x 3 x 4⅝)

65 *Billiard Player III* Plate 30
1945; steel; 71.1 x 58.4 x 16.5 (28 x 23 x 6½)
Neuberger Museum, State University of New York at Purchase, gift of Roy R. Neuberger

66 *Cockfight* Plate 77
1945; steel; 114.5 x 61 x 27.9 (45¹⁄₁₆ x 24 x 11)
Saint Louis Art Museum, purchase (188:1946)

67 *Home of the Welder* Plate 52
1945; steel; 53.3 x 44.1 x 35.6 (21 x 17⅜ x 14)

68 *Steel Drawing I* Plate 57
1945; steel; 56.5 x 66.1 x 15.3 (22¼ x 26 x 6)
Hirshhorn Museum and Sculpture Garden, Washington, D.C.

6. Ibid., roll N.D.D., frame 0299.

This is one of Smith's many representations of the artist and of painting and sculpture studios. Inspired by Picasso's interest in these subjects, Smith executed a number of paintings and sculptures of the artist's studio in the thirties and forties. He elaborated on this theme further in the fifties with portraits of painters, and in the sixties with recreations of the sculptor's workbench.

69 *Cello Player* Plate 43
1946; steel, painted tan; 49.2 x 102.2 x 84.8 (19⅜ x 40¼ x 33⅜); base: 3.5 x 23.8 x 8.9 (1⅜ x 9⅜ x 3½)
David Mirvish, Toronto

70 *Helmholtzian Landscape* Plate 46
1946; steel, painted blue, red, yellow, green, on wooden base; 40.3 x 44.8 x 18.1 (15⅞ x 17⅝ x 7⅛)
Mr. and Mrs. David Lloyd Kreeger, Washington, D.C.

In title, high-key color, expressionistic brushwork, and structure, *Helmholtzian Landscape* is the closest to painting of Smith's many landscape sculptures. Its planar structure, coloring, and the prominence of strongly silhouetted organic form suspended in space prefigure his neo-expressionist landscape paintings of the fifties.

71 *Aggressive Character*
1947; stainless steel, wrought iron on wooden base; 82.6 x 10.2 x 19.1 (32½ x 4 x 7½); base: 4.4 x 17.8 x 21 (1¾ x 7 x 8¼)

72 *Eagle's Lair* Plate 37
1948; steel, bronze; 88.3 x 48.3 x 54 (34¾ x 19 x 21¼)
Rita and Toby Schreiber, Woodside, California

73 *Royal Bird* Plate 82
1948; steel, bronze on stainless steel base; 55.2 x 149.9 x 22.9 (21¾ x 59 x 9)
Walker Art Center, Minneapolis, gift of the T. B. Walker Foundation

Birds — primeval, allegorical, and barnyard — appeared frequently in Smith's works in the forties and fifties. Their prevalence and expressive force indicate their symbolic importance to Smith, as well as their structural fascination for him. His writings reveal his wonder at the evolutionary transition of fish to bird, and he made countless drawings interpreting the close physiognomic relationship between bird and man. *Royal Bird,* the most majestic statement of his avian interest, resembles many other birds by Smith in skeletal silhouette, primal strength, and dynamic suspension of form.

Paintings 1950s

74 *Untitled* (relief construction with two circles) Plate 69
c. 1954; metal, bone, oil, wood, cloth on wood; 65.4 x 85.1
(25¾ x 33½); Estate 75.54.4

Between 1954 and 1957, Smith executed several remarkable series of reliefs, some painted and some sculptural, which are linked by their incorporation of bones or bonelike, organic forms. This particular relief is distinctive in its balance of painterly and sculptural concerns, as well as in the strength of its image. Streaks of red paint add a feeling of violence to the roughly hewn and assembled materials. The combination of wood, metal, bone, and cloth soaked and stiffened in paint has a textural richness characteristic of Smith's reliefs.

75 *Untitled* (four totemic sculptures) Plate 86
1956; oil on canvas; 35.6 x 27.9 (14 x 11); Estate 75.56.15

Smith's first totemic figures were wooden sculptures that he carved in 1933 influenced by African art,[7] but it was not until the fifties that sentinels, totems, and stately personages became a major focus of his work. His delight in pure invention is evident in countless paintings and drawings, such as cat. 96, where groups of similarly shaped and proportioned, but distinctly individual figures are lined up for inspection. Some of these figures actually were or later became sculptures; many more did not. The figures evolved from different arrangements of similar, preselected forms, variously planar, convex/concave, or cubic.

76 *Untitled* (standing woman, profile) Plate 103
1956; oil, enamel on canvas; 182.8 x 44.6 (72 x 17⁹⁄₁₆); Estate 75.56.24

77 *Untitled* (relief with bones) Plate 68
1956; enamel on wood; 27.9 x 40 (11 x 15¾); Estate 80.56.1

This relief combines the immediacy of sculpture with the evocative mystery of painting. Carefully scattered bones are caught up in a swirling vortex of expressionist brushwork reminiscent of the work of Jackson Pollock.

78 *Untitled* (collage for *Fifteen Planes*) Plate 88
1957; paperboard, oil on Masonite; 29.2 x 22.2 (11½ x 8¾); Estate 75.57.22

The cardboard collage that preceded *Fifteen Planes* (fig. 11) is closely related to it in overall design and in most de-

7. When, in 1933–34, David Smith helped John Graham catalog and make bases for Frank Crowninshield's African art collection, he kept some of the pieces in his apartment.

tails; the streaked gray paint approximates the reflective surface of stainless steel. Although Smith used the additive and layering principles of collage in sculpture throughout his career, he executed only a few collages.

79 *Untitled* (neo-impressionist landscape)
1957; oil on canvas; 45.7 x 61 (18 x 24); Estate 75.57.50

80 *Untitled* *(Sentinels)*
1957; oil on Masonite; 40.3 x 52.7 (15⅞ x 20¾); Estate 75.57.5

81 *Untitled* (mountain landscape) Plate 53
c. 1957; oil on Masonite; 19.7 x 61 (7¾ x 24); Estate 75.57.39

All through his career, Smith produced paintings, drawings, and sculptures that reflect the tree-covered, lake-filled landscape of the Adirondacks. In this semiabstract painting, and in his gestural *Cubi XXIII*, 1964 (fig. 9), strong diagonal pattern evokes the underlying rugged dynamism of the mountains surrounding his home in Bolton Landing.

82 *White Egg with Pink* Plate 63
1958; spray paint on canvas; 249.6 x 131.3 (98¼ x 51¾); Estate 75.58.3
Hirshhorn Museum and Sculpture Garden, Washington, D.C., purchase, 1977

Smith's spray paintings and drawings are negative collages. He placed cutout metal and cardboard shapes, found objects, and masking tape onto the canvas (just as he arranged sculptural elements on square white areas on the floor of his shop before welding them). He then sprayed paint around the shapes, coating the surface with up to seven multicolored layers, sometimes shifting the forms slightly between sprays. When the cutout forms and objects were removed, the negative shapes remained silhouetted in clouds of color. The reflective quality of the metallic spray paint that Smith most often used dematerialized the picture surface, paralleling the effect he obtained by burnishing his stainless steel sculptures of the late 1950s and 1960s.

83 *Untitled* (skeletal network) Plate 104
c. 1958; oil and spray paint on linen; 244.5 x 32.4 (96¼ x 12¾); Estate 75.58.27

In some of his spray paintings, Smith highlighted the negative forms with white paint in such a way as to give them the light-reflective tactility characteristic of stainless steel.

84 *Blacksmith Shop*
1959; spray paint on canvas; 237.8 x 24.8 (93⅝ x 9¾); Estate 75.59.31

85 *Chinese Restaurant*
1959; oil on canvas; 257.2 x 127 (101½ x 50); Estate 75.59.16
Philip T. Warren, Coral Gables, Florida

86 *Edgecomb Pond*
1959; spray paint on canvas; 266.7 x 129.5 (105 x 51); Estate 75.59.6
Private collection

87 *Night Window*   Plate 99
1959; spray paint on canvas; 182.9 x 44.8 (72 x 17⅝); Estate 75.59.25

88 *Untitled* (floating galaxy)   Plate 72
c. 1959; spray paint on canvas; 43.2 x 45.7 (17 x 18); Estate 75.59.36

Smith's long-standing ambition to suspend forms in space, free of gravity, was uniquely fulfilled in his spray paintings. This image of limitless space and galactic forms goes far beyond the contained astral projections of *Star Cage,* 1950 (cat. 107).

Drawings 1950s

89 *Chicken Bones*   Plate 79
1951; watercolor, gouache, pen and ink on paper; 46.0 x 58.0 (18⅛ x 22⅞); Estate 73.51.79

Silhouetted like a tree against a stormy sky, this assemblage of bones suggests the close connection with nature in much of Smith's work. It also announces a combination of lateral presentation and elevated gesture that was often repeated in his sculpture of the early fifties, including *Agricola IX,* 1952 (cat. 109), and that was later transformed into such independent statements as *Becca* (cat. 163).

90 *Untitled* (organic abstraction)   Plate 64
1952; gouache, watercolor on paper; 59.4 x 46.4 (23⅜ x 18¼); Estate 73.52.107

91 *Untitled (Tanktotems)*
1952; gouache, watercolor on paper; 46.3 x 59.3 (18¼ x 23⅜); Estate 73.53.2

92 *Untitled* (transparent skull-like sculpture)   Plate 71
1952; watercolor, gouache on paper; 46.2 x 59.3 (18¼ x 23⅜); Estate 73.52.70

This drawing is one of many images in Smith's work of the late forties and fifties that attests to his fascination with bony forms and skeletal structure. Although the drawing has no exact sculptural equivalent, its transparency, fine points of connection, and scattered suspension of forms were incorporated into a number of sculptures, including *Australia,* 1951 (cat. 108), and *Parallel 42,* 1953 (cat. 110).

93 *Untitled* (elevated sculptural form)   Plate 80
1953; gouache, watercolor, ink on paper; 30.5 x 61.0 (12 x 24); Estate 73.53.111

94 *Untitled* (gestural abstraction)
1953; colored ink on paper; 51.8 x 39.6 (20⅜ x 15⅝); Estate 73.53.94

95 *Untitled* (related to *Raven*)   Plate 96
1953; watercolor, gouache on paper; 76.2 x 80.5 (30 x 42¾); Estate 73.53.20

Delicately colored and gestural, this drawing testifies to the expressive range of Smith's art. Although it relates to the *Raven* series (cat. 117), it presents a lyrical evocation of natural form rather than a skeletal diagram of form.

96 *Untitled* (curvilinear sculptures)   Plate 84
c. 1953; ink on paper; 45.6 x 61.1 (18 x 24); Estate 73.53.114

97 *Untitled* (rectangular and cubic sculptures)   Plate 85
c. 1955; watercolor, gouache on paper; 46.0 x 59.1 (18⅛ x 23¼); Estate 73.55.140

This drawing illustrates Smith's method of evolving one sculptural form into another, developing a series of works from different combinations of a particular set of elements. Equally evident is the way in which Smith's sculpture alternates, with only subtle changes, between figural allusion and abstraction. Smith represented a *Cubi* in this watercolor (bottom row, second sculpture) long before he realized one in stainless steel, envisioning from the first the acrobatic, juggling configuration that became characteristic of the sculptural series.

98 *Untitled* (all-over abstraction)
1957; oil, gouache, pencil on paper; 50.9 x 66.5 (20 x 26⅛); Estate 73.57.59

99 *Untitled* (jagged gestural network)
1957; gouache, enamel on paper; 44.3 x 57.3 (17½ x 22½); Estate 73.57.242

100 *Untitled* (mountain landscape)   Plate 55
1957; oil on paper; 40.1 x 50.8 (15¾ x 20); Estate 73.57.110

101 *Untitled* (calligraphy)   Plate 81
1958; ink mixed with egg yolk on paper; 57.5 x 78.4 (22⅝ x 30⅞); Estate 73.58.166

In the fifties, Smith executed hundreds of calligraphic drawings in inks with which he had mixed egg yolk to make them more fluid and translucent. The expressive immediacy and tangibility of this drawing was possibly influenced by Japanese painting, in which, Smith said, "the power intent was suggested by conceiving a stroke outside the paper, continuing through the drawing space to project beyond, so that the included part possessed both power origin and projection. . . . If drops fall, they become acts of providence. If the brush flows dry into hairmarks, such may be greater in energy." [8]

102 *Untitled* (shower of strokes)   Plate 65
1958; ink mixed with egg yolk, oil on paper; 50.4 x 65.4 (19⅞ x 25¾); Estate 73.58.122

Similar in feeling to *Wild Plum,* 1956 (cat. 120), the delicate strokes of this drawing suggest a gentle shower of rain, falling blossoms, or the branches of a weeping willow.

103 *Untitled* (study for *Superstructure on 4)*   Plate 90
1959; spray paint, gouache, pen and ink on paper; 45 x 29 (17¾ x 11⅜); Estate 73.59.119

This working drawing preceded the sculpture's completion by nine months, but its similarity to the final sculpture indicates the precise continuity of Smith's vision. [9] The sculptural form is strongly silhouetted and monumentalized by the spray paint that surrounds it with an illusion of deep space.

104 *Untitled* (figural spray)
c. 1959; spray paint on paper; 44.5 x 29.1 (17½ x 11½); Estate 73.59.114

Photograph 1950s

105 *Untitled* (aerial landscape)
c. 1950–54; photograph; 20.3 x 25.4 (8 x 10)

8. David Smith, "Second Thoughts on Sculpture," *College Art Journal* 13 (Spring 1954): 206.

9. The sculpture is illustrated in Krauss, *Sculpture of David Smith,* no. 493.

Sculpture 1950s

106 *Song of a Landscape*
1950; steel on wooden base; 62.2 x 85.7 x 48.9 (24½ x 33¾ x 19¼)
Muriel Kallis Newman, Chicago

107 *Star Cage*   Plate 73
1950; various metals, painted dark blue; 114.2 x 130.4 x 65.5 (44⅞ x 51¼ x 25¾)
University Gallery, University of Minnesota, Minneapolis, John Rood Sculpture Collection

This work — no doubt inspired by the shimmering, starry patterns in the clear skies above Bolton Landing — is a dynamic diagram of energy, direction, and accent. Its forms are suspended dramatically above the base, giving the illusion of freedom from gravity's constraints.

108 *Australia*   Plate 83
1951; steel, painted brown; 202 x 274 x 41 (79½ x 107⅞ x 16⅛); base: 35.6 (14) diameter
Museum of Modern Art, New York, gift of William Rubin

109 *Agricola IX*   Plate 78
1952; steel; 92.1 x 140.3 x 45.7 (36¼ x 55¼ x 18)

110 *Parallel 42*   Plate 70
1953; steel, painted reddish brown; 135.9 x 66 x 48.3 (53½ x 26 x 19)

Smith's ongoing interest in movement was part of an overall commitment to vitality in art and to expanding the limits of the static media in which he worked. This hanging sculpture — unquestionably influenced by Alexander Calder's mobiles — exemplifies how Smith tried to enhance his sculpture through movement. In spite of its delicate intricacy, the relative lifelessness of *Parallel 42* compared with many other sculptures affirms Smith's greater creativity with implied movement and with illusion of form.

111 *Tanktotem IV*   Plate 97
1953; steel; 235 x 85.1 x 73.7 (92½ x 33½ x 29)
Albright-Knox Art Gallery, Buffalo, gift of Seymour H. Knox, 1957

Moving gingerly across the landscape, *Tanktotem IV* is a gangly messenger from the realm of Smith's imagination. The naturalism inherent in the stature of this figure, the movement suggested by its posture, and the mixed allusions to human and insect form establish its independence as an individual in the world. This figure exudes a punning humor based on the rhythm of the forms, a characteristic of

Smith's finest works with found objects. It belongs to a series of twelve sculptures in which Smith explored the metamorphic possibilities of boiler ends as signifiers of the human anatomy: an intellectually programmatic extension of Picasso's explorations of found objects.

112 *Portrait of a Painter*
1954; bronze; 244.3 x 62.2 x 30.2 (96³⁄₁₆ x 24½ x 11⅞)

113 *Untitled*   Plate 45
1954; steel, painted yellow, lavender, purple, blue, green, black, white, orange, pink; 89.5 x 64.5 x 8.6 (35¼ x 25⅜ x 3⅜)

The gestural basis of Abstract Expressionist painting determined both the form and surface of this sculpture. The dynamic extensions of steel, as well as the de Kooning-esque colors and brushwork give the sculpture the same mixture of awkward intensity and carefully modulated composition that characterized much fifties' painting, including David Smith's. The mannerism evident in this piece, as in a number of other works, is self-conscious, sophisticated, and well chosen. Smith's ongoing rivalry with the acknowledged masters of his lifetime produced fascinating reincarnations of works by Picasso, Giacometti, González, Mondrian, Kandinsky, Pollock, Hofmann, Motherwell, Kline, Noland, and, in this instance, de Kooning.

114 *Forging I*
1955; stainless steel; 173.4 x 12.7 x 2.5 (68¼ x 5 x 1); base: 26.7 (10½) diameter
Rita Ransohoff, New York

115 *Forging IV*
1955; stainless steel; 205.7 x 15.9 x 3.2 (81 x 6¼ x 1¼)

116 *Forging VIII*
1955; stainless steel; 228.6 x 5.7 x 3.2 (90 x 2¼ x 1¼); base: 1.9 x 21.9 x 20.3 (¾ x 8⅝ x 8)

117 *Raven II*   Plate 95
1955; steel, painted black; 64.8 x 109.9 x 23.8 (25½ x 43¼ x 9⅜)

Closely related to his expressionist paintings and drawings, Smith's *Raven* series represents, like Matisse's heads of Jeannette, the evolution of abstract form from a source in the natural world, retaining the formal and emotional essence of the original.

118 *Yellow Vertical*   Plate 105
1955; steel, painted yellow; 235.7 x 42.2 x 36.8 (92¹³⁄₁₆ x 16⅝ x 14½)

Smith's preoccupation with skeletal structure — particularly avian and human — was most evident in paintings, drawings, and sculpture of the fifties. He kept skeletons of birds, cows, and other animals in his house as "objets trouvés" sculpture. He was interested in the elemental forms of these skeletons, but perhaps they also had significance as memento mori for him. *Yellow Vertical,* with its skeletal structure and exploration of the cubist network of line and plane, is related to numerous paintings (cat. 76, 83) and drawings.

119 *Structure 38*
1956; steel; 66 x 66 x 22.9 (26 x 26 x 9)
Janet Bosse, New York

120 *Wild Plum*   Plate 66
1956; silver; 29.2 (11½) diameter

121 *Lonesome Man*   Plate 87
1957; silver; 71.1 x 22.9 x 5.1 (28 x 9 x 2)

122 *Timeless Clock*   Plate 75
1957; silver; 53.3 x 68.6 x 30.5 (21 x 27 x 12)
Mr. and Mrs. Harry W. Anderson, Atherton, California

Comparison of *Timeless Clock* with a drawing related to it (fig. 3) makes clear the way in which Smith transferred to sculpture the clarity, directness, and immediacy that characterized his drawings.

123 *Albany II*
1959; steel, painted black; 55.9 x 47 x 52.1 (22 x 18½ x 20)
William J. Hokin, Chicago

124 *Auburn Queen*   Plate 91
1959; bronze; 219.5 x 93.3 x 54.9 (86⅜ x 36¾ x 21⅝)
Hirshhorn Museum and Sculpture Garden, Washington, D.C.

125 *Study in Arcs*   Plate 106
1959; steel, painted pink; 335.3 x 293.4 x 105.4 (132 x 115½ x 41½); base: 73.3 (28⅞) diameter
Storm King Art Center, Mountainville, New York

Study in Arcs is Smith's purest and most lyrically exuberant extension of painterly gesture out into space. Its pink color reinforces its affirmative expression.

Paintings 1960s

126 *Untitled (Zig VII)* Plate 114
1962; spray paint on canvas; 36.8 x 41.9 (14½ x 16½); Estate 75.62.3

Among Smith's spray paintings and drawings are a number of works that relate to specific sculptures. In the sixties, these pictures of sculptures generally preceded and were studies for their three-dimensional realizations. Such preliminary visions were particularly important since much of Smith's sculpture in the last years of his life was monumental. Like his photographs of his sculpture, these paintings reveal the ideal image of a particular work: the sculpture as David Smith wanted you to see it, as it appeared in his own mind's eye. This painting conveys the free-swinging forms and independent forward propulsion that are the main identifying characteristics of the sculpture *Zig VII.* [10]

127 *Untitled* (flatcar sculpture)
c. 1962; spray paint on canvas; 31.8 x 87 (12½ x 34¼); Estate 75.63.15

128 *Untitled* (free-floating image) Plate 93
c. 1963; oil, spray paint on linen; 47.7 x 69.3 (18¾ x 27¼); Estate 75.63.30

This spray painting is one of many examples in painting and in sculpture of Smith's fascination with floating sculptural forms in space, as free of support as of gravity. Here, the geometric shapes float comfortably within the rectangular field and within the shifting illusionary space created by the layers of spray paint.

129 *Untitled* (overlapping planes) Plate 110
c. 1963; spray paint on canvas; 62.2 x 77.5 (24½ x 30½); Estate 75.63.6
Mr. and Mrs. Kenneth Kaiserman, Philadelphia

A collagelike overlapping of geometric planes was central to Smith's paintings, drawings, and sculptures in the 1960s. The independence and monumentality of the sculptural image in this painting is an easily achieved illusion in two dimensions that is impressive for its small size. One of Smith's greatest achievements in such works as *Becca* (cat. 163) was to transform the art of collage into purely pictorial yet fully three-dimensional sculpture, using thin planes of steel to create an overwhelming impression of presence and scale.

10. Illustrated in ibid., no. 627.

130 *Untitled* (related to *Albany I*)
c. 1963; spray paint on canvas; 45.7 x 50.8 (18 x 20); Estate 75.63. 29

131 *Untitled (Cubi XIX)* Plate 112
1964; spray paint on canvas; 45.7 x 47.6 (18 x 18¾); Estate 75.64.207

Smith's paintings and drawings are often portraits of completed works — as is the case here — or studies for them. This spray painting emphasizes the acrobatic, asymmetrical balance of forms and the unbelievably few points of connection that characterize the actual sculpture (fig. 4). The veils of blue suggest great spatial depth before which the sculptural form rises majestically, while the smears of cream color on the sculpture establish a surface tension that parallels the effect of burnished stainless steel.

132 *Untitled* (green linear nude) Plate 15
c. 1964; enamel on canvas; 62.2 x 99 (24½ x 39); Estate 75.64.111

David Smith drew nudes — always female — in his days at the Art Students League and continued to do so throughout his career. These renderings, which ranged from academic realism to cubist stylization (cat. 17) to Matissian elegance (fig. 5), were distinguished by their directness of presentation and sureness of line. When, in the sixties, Smith transferred his nudes from paper to canvas and ceramics (cat. 151, 152), he created explosive, linear images, expressive of emotion as well as of the speed of their execution.

133 *Untitled* (lavender nude) Plate 19
c. 1964; oil on canvas; 68.6 x 108 (27 x 42½); Estate 75.64.225

134 *Untitled* (rectangular bars) Plate 113
c. 1964; spray paint on canvas; 34.9 x 42.6 (13¾ x 16¾); Estate 75.64.214

135 *Untitled* (seated nude, lower torso) Plate 17
c. 1964; enamel on canvas; 62.2 x 102.2 (24½ x 40¼); Estate 75.64.15

Scale, perspective, and innovative technique make Smith's painted and ceramic nudes radically different from the drawn counterparts he continued to produce in the sixties. Ranging from 23 by 18 to 51 by 44 inches in size, always presenting immediate, closeup views, the nude paintings were poured drawings in the manner of Jackson Pollock, full of intense energy but carefully controlled.

136 *Untitled* (seated nude with raised arm)
c. 1964; enamel on canvas; 84.7 x 69.8 (33⅝ x 27½); Estate 75.64.120

Drawings 1960s

137 *Untitled* (black abstraction) Plate 54
1960; gouache, watercolor on paper; 28.0 x 37.9 (11 x 15); Estate 73.60.206

Smith was always interested in gravity-defying formal relationships and asymmetrical balance, but never more so than in the sixties. This drawing and cat. 138 rival the massively energetic expressionism found in the contemporary paintings of Franz Kline and Robert Motherwell.

138 *Untitled* (color abstraction) Plate 58
1960; watercolor, gouache, enamel on paper; 28.8 x 38.0 (11⅜ x 15); Estate 73.60.205

139 *Untitled* (horizontal sculpture) Plate 92
c. 1960; spray paint, watercolor on paper; 29.1 x 45.0 (11½ x 17¾); Estate 73.60.197

140 *Untitled* (vertical sculpture) Plate 89
1961; spray paint on paper; 44.5 x 29.1 (17½ x 11⁷⁄₁₆); Estate 73.61.60

141 *Untitled* (futurist figure) Plate 98
c. 1961; spray paint on paper; 44.7 x 29.3 (17⅝ x 11½); Estate 73.61.56

142 *Untitled* (two circles)
1962; spray paint on paper; 45.9 x 57.8 (18 x 22¾); Estate 73.62.16

143 *Untitled* (day-glo eclipse) Plate 67
c. 1962; spray paint on paper; 44.9 x 29.1 (17¾ x 11½); Estate 73.62.69

144 *Untitled* (floating color)
c. 1962; spray paint on paper; 45.0 x 29.2 (17¾ x 11½); Estate 73.62.106

145 *Untitled* (floral abstraction) Plate 101
c. 1962; spray paint on paper; 45.1 x 29.2 (17¾ x 11½); Estate 73.62.61

146 *Untitled* (gold-and-rose abstraction)
c. 1962; spray paint on paper; 39.7 x 51.8 (15⅝ x 20⅜); Estate 73.62.167

147 *Untitled* (green-and-gold landscape) Plate 100
c. 1962; spray paint on paper; 44.5 x 55.9 (17½ x 22); Estate 73.62.67

148 *Untitled* (rectangles on sable ground) Plate 74
c. 1962; spray paint on paper; 101.1 x 68.0 (39¾ x 26¾); Estate 73.62.196

This constellation of hard-edge constructivist forms, held together by the same invisible energy that coheres the elements in Smith's sculpture, floats in the immeasurable space created by layers of metallic spray paint.

149 *Untitled* *(2 Circle IV)* Plate 109
c. 1962; spray paint on paper; 44.5 x 29.5 (17½ x 11⅝); Estate 73.63.91

150 *Untitled* (reclining nude) Plate 56
1963; enamel on paper; 44.4 x 57.2 (17½ x 22½);Estate 73.63.41

Ceramics 1960s

151 *Untitled* (nude) Plate 18
1964; clay plate with brown and black glazes and incised design; 34.9 (13¾) diameter; Estate 10

Drawing upon a variety of sources ranging from Cretan pottery to Picasso's ceramics, Smith's ceramic plates are characterized by exquisite fluidity of drawing and vigorously applied color. The surface richness and inventive relation of the figure to its round, gently curving ground make each of his plates distinctive.

152 *Untitled* (nude)
1964; clay plate with black glaze and incised design; 34.9 (13¾) diameter; Estate 8

Sculpture 1960s

153 *Black White Forward* Plate 59
1961; steel, painted black, brown, white; 223.8 x 121.9 x 96.5 (88⅛ x 48 x 38)

Smith experimented with "movement and the color of movement"[11] in many different ways in his sculpture of the 1960s. Here the sculptural surface vibrates from the expressionist brushwork—densely applied though distinctly

11. David Smith Papers, roll N.D.4, frame 0842.

separate black strokes over a dark ground — and from the interplay of black and white planes, which give the illusion of being constantly shifting, with first one toward the viewer and then the other. The suggestion of motion is further extended by the forward tilted posture of the sculpture as a whole, and by the wheels that constitute its base.

154 *Bolton Landing* Plate 94
1961; bronze; 63.8 x 81.7 x 22.2 (25⅛ x 32¼ x 8¾)
Hirshhorn Museum and Sculpture Garden, Washington, D.C.

155 *7 Hours* Plate 34
1961; steel painted black, gray, yellow, blue-black; 214.5 x 122 x 45.5 (84½ x 48⅛ x 18)
Folkwang Museum, Essen, loan from the collection of Reinhard Onnasch, Berlin

156 *Zig IV* Plate 111
1961; steel, painted red-orange, chartreuse; 242.3 x 214 x 193 (95⅜ x 84¼ x 76)
Lincoln Center for the Performing Arts, New York, gift of Mr. and Mrs. Howard Lipman

Belonging among the tableaux that Smith created throughout his career, from the earliest coral still lifes to the *Cubis* of the 1960s, *Zig IV* is the only sculpture whose ground plane is a tilted angle midway between painting and sculpture. The collage elements are arranged at right angles to the ground plane, but they shape space illusionistically and make space tangible, in the same way as do the negative collage forms in Smith's spray paintings.

157 *Voltri I* Plate 102
1962; steel; 235.8 x 56.1 x 48.1 (92⅞ x 22⅛ x 19)
Hirshhorn Museum and Sculpture Garden, Washington, D.C.

158 *Voltri XVI*
1962; steel, 111.8 x 101.6 x 96.5 (44 x 40 x 38)

159 *Menand VI* Plate 107
1963; steel, treated with acid and lacquered; 87 x 51.4 x 43.8 (34¼ x 20¼ x 17¼)
Private collection

The *Agricola, Menand,* and *Albany* series can be seen as small-scale versions of the *Voltri, Cubi,* and *Circle* series. In each case, Smith worked out a particular group of ideas and formal configurations first in table-size sculptures with found objects and prefabricated shapes, and then in monumental sculptures made of industrial parts, some found, such as the *Voltri,* and others made to order. In *Menand VI,* Smith refined the daring concept of juggling abstract, volumetric shapes that distinguishes his greatest *Cubis,* like *Cubi XIX* (fig. 4 and cat. 131).

160 *Volton XIV* Plate 116
1963; steel; 214.9 x 98.4 x 31.8 (84⅝ x 38¾ x 12½)
Anne Mirvish, Toronto

161 *Cubi XII* Plate 117
1963; polished stainless steel; 278.5 x 125.1 x 81.9 (109⅝ x 49¼ x 32¼)
Hirshhorn Museum and Sculpture Garden, Washington, D.C.

162 *Bronze Planes 3/9/64* Plate 108
1964; bronze, silver patina; 42.2 x 64.8 x 10.2 (16⅝ x 25½ x 4)

163 *Becca* Plate 115
1965; stainless steel; 287 x 312.4 x 77.5 (113¼ x 123 x 30½)
Metropolitan Museum of Art, New York, bequest of Adelaide Milton de Groot (1876–1967), by exchange, 1972

Becca is Smith's most complete expression of vitality through gesture. Gestural in form, surface, and content, its Vitruvian extension is unmistakably human in suggestion. Smith once identified the totem in his work as "a yes-statement of a commonly recurring denominator."[12] *Becca* is the ultimate affirmation of that human denominator.

12. McCoy, *David Smith,* p. 178.

Selected Bibliography

For a comprehensive bibliography through 1965, see Krauss, *Sculpture of David Smith* (1977). This has been expanded and continued through 1979 in Cummings, *David Smith: The Drawings.*

Carandente, Giovanni. *Voltron: David Smith.* Philadelphia: Institute of Contemporary Art, University of Pennsylvania, 1964.

Cone, Jane Harrison. *David Smith 1906–1965.* Exhibition catalog. Boston: Fogg Art Museum, Harvard University, 1966.

Cummings, Paul. *David Smith: The Drawings.* Exhibition catalog. New York: Whitney Museum of American Art, 1979.

David Smith Papers, loaned to the Archives of American Art, Smithsonian Institution, Washington, D.C., by Candida and Rebecca Smith.

Fry, Edward F. *David Smith.* Exhibition catalog. New York: Solomon R. Guggenheim Museum, 1969.

Gray, Cleve, ed. *David Smith by David Smith.* New York: Holt, Rinehart and Winston, 1968.

Krauss, Rosalind E. *Terminal Iron Works: The Sculpture of David Smith.* Cambridge, Mass.: MIT Press, 1971.

——. *The Sculpture of David Smith: A Catalogue Raisonné.* New York and London: Garland Publishing, 1977.

McClintic, Miranda. *David Smith: The Hirshhorn Museum and Sculpture Garden Collection.* Exhibition catalog. Washington, D.C.: Smithsonian Institution Press, 1979.

McCoy, Garnett, ed. *David Smith.* New York: Praeger Publishers, 1973.

Wilken, Karen. *David Smith: The Formative Years.* Exhibition catalog. Edmonton, Alberta: Edmonton Art Gallery, 1981.

Photography Credits

Dan Budnik, New York: pages 6–7, 17, 19, 46–47; Geoffrey Clements, Staten Island, N.Y.: plate 35; Ken Cohen, New York: plates 61, 65, 76, 93, 104 and fig. 1; Ali Elahi, New York: plate 89; M. Lee Fatherree, San Francisco: plate 37; David Finn, New York: plate 106; George Fletcher, Des Moines: plate 21; Fogg Art Museum, Harvard University: fig. 5; Bruce C. Jones, Rocky Point, N.Y.: plate 31; Los Angeles County Museum of Art (Contemporary Art Council Fund): fig. 9; Robert McAfee: page 2; A. Mewbourn, Bellaire, Texas: plate 49; David Mirvish Gallery, Toronto: plate 43; National Gallery of Art, Washington, D.C.: fig. 6; Sammlung Reinhard Onnasch, Berlin: plate 34; Alfred Puhn, San Francisco: page 131; T. K. Rose, New York: plates 19, 27, 39, 51, 53, 55, 100, 101, 111; Garth Sheuer, Toronto: cover, plate 116; David Smith (courtesy Candida and Rebecca Smith and the Archives of American Art): plates 1, 8, 30, 33, 48, 52, 70, 75, 78, 82, 83, 87, 94, 95, 97, 107, 108, 110, 115, and figs. 4, 7, 8, 11; David Smith Papers, Archives of American Art: pages 4–5, 11, 25; William Soghor, New York: plate 26; Lee Stalsworth, Hirshhorn Museum and Sculpture Garden: plates 9, 20, 29, 41, 42, 48, 54, 56, 67, 71, 80, 84, 85, 90, 92, 98, 109, and figs. 2, 3, 10; Bettina Sulzer, New York: plate 16; John Tennant, Hirshhorn Museum and Sculpture Garden: plates 2–7, 10–13, 15, 17, 18, 23–25, 28, 29, 32, 36, 40, 44–47, 50, 57, 58, 60, 62–64, 66, 68, 69, 72, 74, 79, 81, 86, 88, 91, 96, 99, 102, 103, 105, 112–14, 117; University Gallery, University of Minnesota, Minneapolis: plate 73; Louise Walker, Saint Louis Art Museum: plate 89.